A Time to Laugh—
A Time to Cry

Bonnie Wasser

NORTHWESTERN PUBLISHING HOUSE
Milwaukee, Wisconsin

Other titles especially for women:

Blessings by the Handful by Rachel Tacke
The Gift of Prayer by Jane Schenvogt
Sweet the Moments by DeLyn Wagenknecht

Library of Congress Control Number: 2004107739
Northwestern Publishing House
1250 N. 113th St., Milwaukee, WI 53226-3284
www.nph.net
© 2004 Northwestern Publishing House
Published 2004
Printed in the United States of America
ISBN 0-8100-1690-7

There is a time for everything . . .
a time to weep
and a time to laugh.
Ecclesiastes 3:1,4

May the words of my mouth
and the meditation of my heart
be pleasing in your sight, O LORD,
my Rock and my Redeemer.
Psalm 19:14

Contents

Editor's Preface

For Martin Luther the female perspective was deserving of great admiration. "Earth has nothing more tender," he wrote, "than a woman's heart when it is the abode of piety."

How remarkably true and wise! Women perceive life in a way that is profoundly different from a man's understanding. Sometimes the differences are subtle. At other times a woman's viewpoint stands in bold juxtaposition to a male's view. Subtle or stark, a woman's view on life is inevitably unique because it uses the human heart as its filter.

This book is part of an effort to give voice to the expressions of godly women in every walk and stage of life. The purpose of this book and others like it is to examine the great themes and important struggles that are part of every Christian woman's experience—to help her explore her blessings, examine her faith, inspire her family, endure her suffering, excel in her prayer life, and become fully engaged in the worship of her Savior-God.

In a world gone giddy with the ideology of radical feminism, these books written by women and for women provide a meaningful dialogue bathed in the light of God's eternal Word. May the give and take of these timeless conversations bring glory to God's holy name and a rich harvest of blessings to this book's readers.

Kenneth J. Kremer, editor

Introduction

During our 41 years of marriage, Bob and I have been blessed with 25 children. Three sons came to us by birth. Four Korean-born daughters joined our family by adoption. Then we thought our family was complete, until we became aware of the many older children waiting in legal limbo here in the United States. We planned to add one more son . . . and did, but the Lord used that adoption to add another son, then daughters and more daughters, then two more sons, until suddenly—well, to us it seemed like suddenly—our family included 25 sons and daughters.

Since 1981 we have usually had eight children under the age of 18 in our home, plus a couple of adult "kids" going to college or looking for jobs. Today we have only four at home. Soon our nest will be empty. Will we be lonely when that happens? Unlikely. We'll have grandchildren.

Our family was built through the adoption process. But this book is not really about adoption. Rather, it is about the personal struggles in my daily spiritual life. Over the years I've discovered that people identify with me, whether they have adopted children or not. So I have gathered my musings, mutterings, and memories into this collection. Jesus Christ is at the center of it all. When faced with both the trivial concerns of life as well as traumatic events, he is my rock, my peace, my hope. My purpose is to encourage others with his strength. It's my hope and constant prayer that God will use the words in each chapter to give others a time to laugh, a time to cry, and a time to move closer to him. It's the best way I know to share my faith. In this way, *A Time to Laugh—A Time to Cry* will bring glory to God's name.

> There is a time for everything,
> and a season for every activity under heaven:
> a time to be born and a time to die,
> a time to plant and a time to uproot,
> a time to kill and a time to heal,
> a time to tear down and a time to build,
> a time to weep and a time to laugh,
> a time to mourn and a time to dance,
> a time to scatter stones and a time to gather them,
> a time to embrace and a time to refrain,
> a time to search and a time to give up,
> a time to keep and a time to throw away,
> a time to tear and a time to mend,
> a time to be silent and a time to speak,
> a time to love and a time to hate,
> a time for war and a time for peace.
>
> Ecclesiastes 3:1-8

CHAPTER ONE

That Word *Wait!*

The other day I heard myself tell one of my kids, "Not right now. You'll have to wait." I don't recall the circumstances, but I remember the word and the trouble it can cause. *Wait* is a worse word than *no*. At least with *no*, it's settled. But, *wait?* A lot of things can happen with *wait*.

Perhaps the most difficult wait in my life was when we were adopting our first two daughters—five-year-old Sari and two-year-old Heidi.

We waited for 18 months to be "matched" with Sari and Heidi, sisters from Korea. Being matched meant we had two little black and white pictures, showing these two rather serious looking girls, dressed in mismatched outfits that were obviously too big. We thought they were the most beautiful little girls we had ever seen. The next three months were spent wading through a mountain of immigration paperwork to get their visas so they could come to the United States. The visas finally arrived, and on December 3 we got that special phone call from the international adoption agency, saying the girls would be arriving at O'Hare airport in one week.

One week! Eighteen months of waiting, and now we were down to a week. We bought feminine, furry winter coats for both girls. The adoption papers said the girls liked fruit, so we stocked the refrigerator with fresh fruit. We set up two new beds, complete with ruffled bedspreads from our neighbors. Then we phoned everyone we could think of to share our joy and excitement. And in every conversation we praised the Lord for answering our prayers and bringing our two girls home for Christmas.

Five days later the adoption agency called again: "The girls won't be coming after all. They have chicken pox. With the heavy Christmas traffic, we have no idea when we'll be able to get them on another flight."

My maternal instincts kicked in. My daughters were sick. They belonged here where their new mother and father could care for them, not halfway around the world. "God, why are you allowing this to happen?"

I was angry—angrier than I can remember being in my whole life. I was also afraid I might never see the daughters who were already loved by all of us. It wasn't fair! Didn't God care anymore?

I'm one of those people who cries when she's happy, cries when she's sad, cries when she's overwhelmed, and cries when she's mad. In one way or another, I was all of the above. Thus began my marathon of tears. My husband, Bob, tried to calm me, but it did little good. My evening was spent crying.

That night I concentrated on crying quietly so Bob could sleep. By 2 A.M. I realized my pillow was soggy. I felt dehydrated, empty; so I got up to get a drink. Standing in the dark with just enough light to catch my shadowy reflection in the mirror, I had the thought that if I continued to let my emotions get the best of me, my daughters wouldn't have a stable mother to come home to. Neither would our sons.

When I returned to our bedroom, I saw Bob's Bible on the nightstand. In the past, its words always gave me comfort. But I couldn't remember ever feeling this devastated. I carried the book into the girls' waiting bedroom. Two beautiful bedspreads with matching curtains and two soft dolls waited patiently. Between the sobs I began to pray. "All right, God. You've allowed the girls to get the chicken pox, which means they can't come until the scabs are healed because they'd never get through immigration at the airport. But why couldn't you put it off a few days?"

He didn't answer. I felt worse.

I finally opened the Bible . . . not to the New Testament as is my usual habit. Rather I opened it to the Old Testament and

2

prayed, "Lord, you probably aren't ready to give me an answer quite yet . . . especially after the way I've been acting. However, I can't go on like this. I can't live without hope." It dawned on me that by turning my back on God in anger, I had also turned my back on his hope.

The text I had randomly opened to in my Bible was 2 Chronicles 7:12. God was talking to Solomon about the building of the temple. "I have heard your prayer," said the Lord, "and have chosen this place for myself as a temple for sacrifices." This night the Lord's words were meant to give me hope and strengthen my faith. God was saying to me: "Wait. It will be worth all the disappointment." Not no, but rather wait.

I had prayed in anger and bitterness, but the Lord took pity on me. I had learned that to reject God and to try to live without him was like tasting the hopelessness of hell.

Waiting is still hard sometimes. But it gets easier when I remember waiting for Sari and Heidi. As it says in Psalm 33:20-22: "We wait in hope for the LORD; he is our help and our shield. In him our hearts rejoice, for we trust in his holy name. May your unfailing love rest upon us, O LORD, even as we put our hope in you." When the Lord says wait, it simply means he wants to fill us up with hope first.

CHAPTER TWO

A Lesson
about Lemons

The year after Sari and Heidi arrived from Korea—making us a large family of three boys and two girls—we thought our family was complete.

We continued to thank the Lord for our five blessings and eagerly shared their stories and ours at every opportunity. These opportunities were a fairly regular occurrence because the rather odd look of our family led to questions. The girls had their Asian black hair and beautiful almond-shaped eyes. Two of our sons were like me, blue-eyed blondes. The oldest was Bob's image with brown eyes and brown hair. It was a wonderful time in our family's life.

The only challenge of those years was a decline in profits from our family-owned businesses. Once thriving, things began to change as the inflation of the '70s grew and interest rates rose. When the interest rates for business loans and mortgages hit 18 percent, we were forced to struggle to live even more frugally than normal.

We hit bottom on the day a mechanic told Bob to consider junking our "new" car, though it only had 44,000 miles on it.

At 30,000 miles, we'd had an expensive valve job done. Now, just 14,000 miles later, it needed another valve job. The car was a lemon. Getting another car made sense. Getting the lemon fixed again was only throwing good money after bad. Except, there was no money—good or bad.

Bob was down that night when he told me the bad news. Then three-year-old Heidi discovered he was home and greeted him with the happy words "Daddy's home!"

How quickly our perspective changed! Bob gave his dark-haired, almond-eyed daughter a huge bear hug and swung her in his arms while I went to fix supper. When the other kids arrived, six hungry voices would be asking, "What's for dinner?"

I found myself wondering if the Lord was allowing Satan to test our faith a bit. We'd been very outspoken telling others that God was the reason we had our beautiful family. How else but by God's grace could we ever have gotten two beautiful daughters from halfway around the world? Was it possible Satan expected us to stop praising God if money became scarce?

Well, money was scarce. Being self-employed, we had no set income. The gas bill—due in a week—already had a shut off notice attached. The electric bill was due three days later. The car insurance, right after that. Plus, somehow we had to eat and pay the mortgage . . . after we had paid our employees. And now it looked as though we would be facing either another huge repair bill or monthly car payments again.

I reminded myself of the verses in Matthew chapter 6: "So do not worry, saying, 'What shall we eat?' or 'What shall we drink?' or 'What shall we wear?' For the pagans run after all these things, and your heavenly Father knows that you need them" (verses 31,32). I envisioned myself handing over the keys of our broken car to the Lord.

That night I impulsively reminded Rob, our oldest, "Don't forget to ask God to fix our car in your prayers tonight."

His eleven-year-old's reply was indignant: "Pray for a car? That's dumb. God doesn't fix cars."

"God can fix anything he wants," I said, "using whatever method he chooses. He does care about our car, Rob. He knows we need it." The look on Rob's face told me he was skeptical.

The next morning on our drive to church, the car seemed to be telling us how bad things really were. The motor quit at every stop sign and roughly putt-putted down the road whenever it chose to work. As we reached church, I suggested we all include the car in our prayers that day. Sari, Heidi, and seven-year-old Steve nodded. Rob, nine-year-old Craig, and Bob gave me skeptical but tolerant looks.

Two hours later, as we headed home, the motor was running even worse. I began to pray a new prayer: "God, please get us home before it quits."

We had a big breakfast that Sunday morning. For a while food took thoughts and conversation off the car and all of the attending problems connected with our financial crisis. Then, without warning, it all came bubbling back to the surface. In sheer frustration, Bob pushed his chair back and said: "Maybe I'll take another look at that engine. I just have a feeling we're missing something."

My response was "You look. I'll pray!"

The kids took turns shuttling back and forth from the house to the car and back again, making a progress report with each trip. When I felt Bob's patience should just about be spent, I decided to take up my position at his side in a posture of resignation and support. I really had nothing else to offer in the way of advice or mechanical knowledge.

But as I approached the car, Bob popped out from under the hood, grinning. "Take a look at this," he said. "I just found it." He held up an array of wires, singled out one, and asked, "Know what this is?"

I swallowed my "Of course not" and just shook my head.

"Distributor cap. Compare it with this one." He held up another set of wires.

The difference was obvious. "There's a piece missing," I said. Giddy with new confidence at having actually recognized that something was not right with the first set of wires, I asked, "Would a bad distributor cap ruin the valve?"

"It would make the car run rough. It could explain the first valve job. The motor couldn't run right in that cylinder. This car probably came from the factory this way."

"How much to fix it?" I asked, hesitantly.

"Maybe all of $25," he said, smiling broadly.

In the years that have followed, I have been reminded often of the Lord's total caring when it comes to our needs. Our financial problems didn't immediately disappear with the replacement of a distributor cap. But my attitude changed.

Seven years and 60,000 miles later, that lemon became Rob's as he drove it to college. The day he was to leave for school, I couldn't resist asking, "Think we should pray for the Lord to take care of your car?"

"You'd better," he said. "I have a long way to drive it yet."

Since that day I've had many thing to be concerned about, but Matthew 10:30 always reminds me of God's loving care and concern. That's the verse that says "the very hairs of your head are all numbered." In my case that would include all the gray hairs.

CHAPTER THREE

Do Not Worry . . .

Some drivers panic when they hear a rattle in their cars. In ours we figure it's one of the kids' missing possessions . . . and hope it isn't a gerbil.

Early in our marriage, when we only had five kids, I probably would have insisted Bob do a thorough check to find the source of our new noise. Not knowing conjured up possibilities. Maybe the muffler system had lost a clamp. Or worse, a wheel might be loose. Or worse yet, the bottom of the car might be falling off.

Three years after Sari and Heidi joined our family, we asked to be considered as a family for another little girl, this time one who didn't have a lot of options for being placed. A short time later we received a call from the international agency. They had two sisters from Korea who were not going to be able to stay with the family that had originally planned to adopt them. Would we consider making them a part of our family? This wasn't going to be a routine foreign adoption because we would have to drive to the East Coast where the girls were now living in a foster home. We would meet them, learn more about them, and hopefully bring them back home with us.

We said yes. To make it easier for our "new" daughters (as we now thought of them), we decided to take our five other sons and daughters, assuming the new kids would relate more easily to the "old" kids than they would be able to relate to adults. We also felt the old ones would more readily bond with the new ones if they were all part of the assimilation process. There was one problem. On such short notice, where would we get our traveling money?

We explained to the old kids that we weren't going to have any extra money for "doing things." In fact, we really weren't sure where we would get the money we had to have for gas and motels. They, of course, put everything in perspective by reminding us that if God wanted us to go, he'd give us what we needed.

I began baking muffins and cookies and carefully planned how we would fill our coolers with boiled eggs, carrot sticks, sandwiches, tomatoes from our garden, cheese, juice, and milk. And for those with Asian tastes—Bob, Sari, and Heidi—pickles. In another container we put cereal measured into individual servings, boxes of crackers, peanut butter, jelly, and a good assortment of the cookies and muffins.

We were still very short of actual cash. We had always been cautious about using credit cards but decided we would use one card for buying gas. Then, on the day before we were scheduled to leave, a check arrived in the mail from a publisher who wanted to reprint one of my stories. The credit was undeniably the Lord's. The amount of the check covered the cost of the gas, the motels, and a little extra food on the way.

That unexpected check demonstrated the futility of worry. We are more precious to the Lord than the birds of the air that do not sow or reap or store up their food. "Therefore do not worry about tomorrow, for tomorrow will worry about itself. Each day has enough trouble of its own" (Matthew 6:34).

About halfway out to the coast Bob and I posed a question to our kids: What if that check hadn't come? They concluded wisely that it really wouldn't have mattered. God would have found another way.

Watching for Miracles

"He performs wonders that cannot be fathomed, miracles that cannot be counted." These are Job's words (5:9). I wonder what Job considered a miracle.

One has to be careful these days in calling an event a miracle. The norm is to rationalize everything. And for those occasions when rationalizing doesn't work, the word *coincidence* is applied. There are some similarities. *Miracle* as defined by Webster is an event that appears to be unexplainable by the laws of nature and thus is attributed to God. *Coincidence* is defined as a remarkable occurrence of events, apparently happening by mere chance.

Thinking back, there have been times when mere chance just didn't seem to fit. For example, there was the time shortly after we had been blessed with our eighth child, a 13-year-old boy named Scott.

Scott had been waiting for a *forever* family since he was two years old. Now that he had a permanent home and a real family, he sometimes didn't know what to do with us. We understood that things were very different for him. He was now attending a Lutheran elementary school rather than the special program he'd been part of in the public school system. My routine was to stop and talk with his teacher each afternoon.

One day Scott's teacher said that he was permitting Scott to take a social studies test home to make corrections. Scott had done poorly on the test; this was a chance to improve his grade.

When I asked Scott to show me the test paper, he said he didn't have it. He'd lost it.

Our son Steve reached into a wastebasket in the corner of the classroom and pulled out a couple sheets of paper. "Here it is," he said.

Scott bolted for the door and disappeared.

"Want me to go after him?" asked Steve.

"Take his jacket and try," I said to Steve. This was Wisconsin, and it was January.

The teacher and I stood by the window and watched Steve cross the playground toward the woods. At the edge he stopped, still holding Scott's winter jacket, shaking his head.

The next hour was spent looking . . . calling . . . searching. After an hour, Steve joined us in the car for a while to get warm. I could only wonder how cold Scott was. At that point, I knew instinctively that we were going to have to involve the police. It was too dangerous for Scott to be out in weather this cold, unprotected. I parked the car to make it more visible from several directions. And I started to wonder how I might make contact with the police without leaving the area.

It was then that I saw a city squad car one block ahead of us. Now the problem was to try to stop a police car driving ahead of us. We prayed for help.

The police car pulled into the church parking lot. My first thought was that the teacher had called. I pulled up next to the squad and jumped out to explain our situation. The officer called in our request.

Steve, now warm, got back out and started looking on foot again. I made another pass near the woods in the car. Fifteen minutes later we saw Steve holding on to his new brother behind the school. Scott was still struggling.

"I wasn't going to let him get away," said Steve. "I'm getting cold again. And hungry."

We both held on to the newest member of our family. The teacher went to get Scott's jacket. When he returned we told Scott we'd let go so he could get his jacket on if he promised not to run again.

"Need help?" called the officer from his squad car.

"No, I think it's okay now," I called back. I must have looked a little silly practically sitting on top of Scott.

The officer waved. I murmured a "thanks" that he probably couldn't hear and waved back.

We let Scott up and got him into his jacket. Then together we walked back through the school to pick up his backpack and the social studies test. The car ride home was quiet, uneventful, and warm.

Amazingly, Scott had no signs of frostbite. But he was pretty dirty from hiding under bushes, shivering from the cold.

At the time we thought of this event as a miracle. Thinking back, we still do but in a way different from what we first thought. What happened to Scott on that day actually became a sign of what permanence in our family meant. We had not sent him back . . . or even called the social worker to talk about Scott's behavior. To us, the miracle was that God had provided an opportunity to demonstrate our love to Scott. It also showed us that God was willing to help us parent a young man with scars from his past. Scott is his child too.

This wasn't our last miracle with Scott. In fact, watching for miracles became a routine part of parenting Scott. And later with other kids as well, we often echoed Job's sense of awe as he gave glory to God, because "he performs wonders that cannot be fathomed, miracles that cannot be counted."

CHAPTER FIVE

The Inheritance

When our family gathers and the kids start telling stories, I have the fear that someday one of them might write a book. Is it possible to add a clause to one's will that restricts heirs from writing such a book? Perhaps I could prime the pump by bribing would-be authors with the promise of inheritance money. At this point though it's looking like there won't be much incentive there, considering an inheritance split 25 ways.

Maybe I should simply beat them to it. Telling stories, I mean.

A favorite story of the three sisters we adopted at ages 11 (twins) and 14 is about the time that Mom got angry with Dad and went to sleep in the living room. As I recall, someone had broken my new music box and wouldn't confess, and Dad wasn't as sympathetic as he should have been.

This was the first time these three girls had heard us react in anger toward each other. They panicked, got out of bed, and packed up all their belongings. They were sure that their happy new home wasn't so happy after all and was about to break up.

The next morning all three arose early, met in the hallway, and crept downstairs to see if Mom was gone. Nope. She was still there, sleeping on the living room couch. And on the other living room couch lay Dad!

As he explained it to them later, if Mom wouldn't come back upstairs, then he would stay downstairs with her.

The three sisters decided that maybe this was going to be a good *forever* home anyway. They headed back upstairs, unpacked, and returned to bed.

The Lord used our disagreement to give our new daughters a sense of security.

Another favorite is the story of Dad's pet goose, named Duck, who waited for Dad to come home every night and would greet his "Hey, Duck," with a "Honk, honk." (Duck also liked to sunbathe with the girls. But that's another story.)

The older kids like to talk about getting up on winter mornings to have hot, freshly baked coffee cakes for breakfast. It wasn't that they had a June Cleaver–type mom but, rather, that I was usually behind on deadlines for articles and stories and was up early to work on them. Their father doesn't think any part of the house should be heated unless it's being used. The fastest way to warm up the kitchen, where the typewriter was, was to bake something.

As I think again about writing that will, there is really only one thing that matters, one thing that I want my children to inherit: the desire to serve the Lord in whatever they do. If they do, my life's dream will be fulfilled. As Peter says in Colossians 3:23,24, "Whatever you do, work at it with all your heart, as working for the Lord, not for men, since you know that you will receive an inheritance from the Lord as a reward. It is the Lord Christ you are serving." That's the legacy I want to leave to my children.

And if someone decides to write a book, I'm hoping it will be dedicated to Christ, for his use and to his glory.

CHAPTER SIX

Those Noisy Kids
in the Back Pew

He wouldn't sit still, he couldn't keep quiet, and every 20 seconds he would ask, "Go home now?" Finally, I took him outside and gave him a swat on the seat—and then looked up to see a police officer, sitting in his squad car—watching me.

I've told that story about the humility of coping with a noisy toddler in church often. Parents usually identify with me and then add some humbling stories of their own. Some are funny; a few are sad. The saddest, though, are the ones that end: "Then I was told I shouldn't bring my kids to church because they disrupt the service. What should I do? If we don't bring them, how will they learn? But we don't want them to spoil things for everyone else either."

This is not a new problem. It's been going on as long as parents have been bringing their kids to church.

Last Sunday we happened to sit near the back—the only pew long enough for all of us—in front of a two-year-old, a four-year-old, and their father. Periodically, there were rumblings behind us. At one point an obviously exasperated dad said firmly, "No. You'll have to wait."

I must admit I let my mind imagine what they were waiting for. Yet I also must say that the distraction did not take away from my personal worship. Why? Because I was reminded that Jesus had himself rebuked his disciples and taken the time to receive the little children who were being brought to him. "Let the little children come to me," he said, "and do not hinder

17

them, for the kingdom of heaven belongs to such as these" (Matthew 19:14). Then he blessed them.

Perhaps, like the disciples, we must learn how to be a little more patient with children when parents bring them to the Lord's house. After all, children have the kind of faith that Jesus considered admirable. "I tell you the truth, anyone who will not receive the kingdom of God like a little child will never enter it" (Luke 18:17). God wants us to approach him with an unquestioning, childlike faith.

Christ also spoke about adult attitudes toward children: "See that you do not look down on one of these little ones" (Matthew 18:10). And in Mark 9:37, we read, "Whoever welcomes one of these little children in my name welcomes me." Perhaps that is what back-pew sitters, like us, need to remember: in welcoming these children we are welcoming the Lord.

One thing I've noticed over the years, the children sitting in the back pews change. They grow. Their parents become braver and move forward. Then other moms and dads with little ones take their places.

I no longer have any of those noisy kids in the back pew. But when I realize how precious children are to our Lord, I'm thankful that other parents are bringing theirs. I'm also grateful that I'm not the one needing to keep order or apologize to the people sitting nearby.

CHAPTER SEVEN

The Perfect Father

He only scolds when it's needed. He only raises his voice to be heard. He only gets angry when others fail to listen. He listens even when he'd rather be reading the Sunday paper. He stops mowing the lawn just to talk. He wakes up from his after-dinner nap to give his opinion on what movie to watch tonight on TV.

He makes enough money so there's always a roof over your head and plenty of food on the table, even if it isn't always pizza. He doesn't make so much money that he's tempted to write out blank checks, which means you have to learn to set priorities about what you really need and what you think you really need.

He likes every one of his kids. And even though at times you feel a little in awe of him, you also feel you are special just because you are one of his kids. The awe you feel may be responsible for some pretty big decisions that you've made over the years—decisions like "I will not shoplift because if I'm caught my father will kill me" and "No, I won't go to that beer party because if my father catches me driving his car when I've had something to drink, he'll not only kill me, he'll never let me drive again!"

He's a father who's not afraid to tell you when he's made a mistake, even if it takes him three years to discover it. He is not afraid to reconsider your punishment if he has made a mistake, which means your lifetime grounding might be rolled back to six years any day now.

He teaches you to drive, even when you've pulled out in front of an oncoming car, run a stop sign, gone over the speed limit, and hit the curb with his new whitewall tires.

He admits that he wasn't perfect in his youth. And he admits this on the day you get your first F on an exam. But then he says you can't go out with your friends tonight because it's a school night and, after all, you don't want to get another F tomorrow.

He lets you dream about what you'd like to be when you're out of school—and then reminds you that biochemists should pass their science courses. The next day he hands you an article from the newspaper stating how biochemists are going to be in demand in the next ten years and then says, "Go for it."

He doesn't tell you how to live your life, but he shows a good route to take by his own example. He didn't take you to Sunday school; he went with you and for a time was your teacher. He didn't drop you off at church services; he held you by the hand, and together the two of you walked to the front pew, where you could see better and where you promised to behave.

Yes, you have known for years that your dad is a good dad. He's never been afraid to share his belief in the triune God, and he's never hesitated to share the truth that there is only one perfect father—the Father who "so loved the world that he gave his one and only Son, that whoever believes in him shall not perish but have eternal life" (John 3:16).

No, your dad isn't a perfect father. But the reason he is a good dad is because he's always trying to walk in the perfect Father's footsteps.

On Father's Day it's nice to say thanks for both!

CHAPTER EIGHT

The Planters

Ours is not always an ideal family. Nor would I ever want to give the impression that it is.

Picture this: I am a mother of many children, confined to crutches and the couch, with a compound fractured leg that is held together with metal pins, plates, and rods. One daughter has recently been enrolled in a faraway boarding school for her final semester of high school in order to distance her from the street gang that used her to transport their illegal drugs. Another daughter is living with friends an hour's drive away to protect her from the repeated threats of the same gang that wants to find her older sister. It's Easter evening. I'm resting on the couch from a busy day, waiting for Dad to return from taking our sophomore daughter back to our friends' home. It should have taken him two hours in driving time and one hour of visiting time. Four and a half hours have now passed since he left. With gang threats on our family, it's difficult not to worry. I find myself praying for his safety.

Another half hour passes before Bob returns. When he finally arrives, his first words are "I know what I want to do with the rest of my life."

The first thing that comes to my mind is "What's wrong with what you're doing now?" But before I have a chance to utter a single word, he has already proclaimed, "We are going to build a boarding school for kids in crisis."

He kept talking. I was still back at the *we*.

All I ever wanted to do in life was to marry Bob, have a couple of kids, and write. And it all happened, but not necessarily in the way I had imagined. I'm married to Bob, have 25 kids, and write—when I can wedge in a half-hour block of time. I've learned to be careful about how those precious blocks of time are used.

As Bob continued to sketch out plans for what eventually would become Calvary Academy—a boarding school for kids in crisis—I was working hard, thinking of ways to let *him* do it.

First, I concluded, this was an idea that Bob shared with some of our friends. I was not a principal party in creating the vision.

Second, at that exact moment, a broken leg was limiting my energy and mobility.

Third—I couldn't think of a third, but given time I would.

Then I permitted myself to listen to Bob's enthusiastic plans. The school would be a Christian boarding school. Christian witnessing would surround the kids 24 hours a day. The staff would consist of caring Christians willing to share their faith and live their faith as an example to kids who were hurting. Following the Fourth Commandment, we would be supportive of the family and an extension of the parents, as our authority would come through them. As a proactive program, parents would enroll their kids before the juvenile court system became an adjudicated part of the children's lives. The program would focus on kids whose behaviors were already too difficult to live with in a family setting, school setting, or community setting.

I understood what Bob was talking about. In addition to the daughter now trying to put her life back together at a distant school, we'd had another daughter, adopted at age 14, who at 16 ran away from our home. We figured it was because she'd been kicked out of so many homes before, she felt she might as well start living on her own before we kicked her out of ours. The question for us was how could we keep her safe and continue to show her we loved her? We tried; she ran. We tried harder; she ran farther.

We sought help through social services and the courts and placed her in a secular residential treatment center that came highly recommended. There she learned how to become independent. Of course, our purpose was never to force her to remain dependent into adulthood. But we did want her to know how much we love her and that she could turn to us for help any time she needed it. We also wanted her to know that our love for her was a reflection of her Savior's love. We wanted her to know that Jesus provides healing and peace and that running away from one's problems resolves nothing. But the secular treatment center continued talking about independence.

When I think about this daughter, now an adult, I grieve for her relationships—with us and with Christ—that today are so much weaker than we had once hoped they would be. I find myself wondering what else we might have done. How can loving parents help their child make safe choices? How can godly moms and dads help their child continue to grow closer to the Lord when all the child seems to want is independence at any cost, even at the cost of eternal life? As parents we desperately want to teach our children that Jesus loves them and died for them to wash all of their sins away, that he wants them to spend eternity with him in heaven. But what does a parent do when the child refuses to listen and becomes determined to follow a more worldly path?

The world of social services and the courts is set up to send children in crisis to court-ordered residential treatment centers. By law, these centers are required to separate church and state. If they fail to do so, they will lose their federal and state funding. Sending a rebellious child to such a place is guaranteeing that grace and faith and God's love and forgiveness are not part of the healing process. No matter what the caseworkers' personal beliefs may be, it is a given that they will refrain from sharing those beliefs.

So where else can parents go for help when a rebellious child needs to find safety and take time to heal?

The answer came through loud and clear as Bob continued to describe his dream. "Calvary Academy will keep the kids safe while providing each of them with the opportunity to hear God's Word every day. We'll plant the seed; the Holy Spirit will make it grow."

Bob's words ran parallel to something Saint Paul once wrote: "The Lord has assigned to each his task. I planted the seed, Apollos watered it, but God made it grow. So neither he who plants nor he who waters is anything, but only God, who makes things grow. . . . For we are God's fellow workers" (1 Corinthians 3:5-9).

Maybe I don't need to come up with a third excuse. Remembering Paul's words, my first two excuses don't seem as important anymore either. Actually, it's a privilege to be part of the "we," wherever it takes me. Of course, in my opinion, it would be nice if writing were part of it. In any case, though, my prayer will continue to be "Lord, please make me good at planting or watering or whatever other tasks you might have in mind for me."

CHAPTER NINE

The Reluctant Worker

"The heart is willing, but the body is weak." My grandmother used to say this when one of us would ask her to play a game like baseball or king of the hill. As my 60th birthday comes closer, there are more and more occasions when I understand her sentiments.

For me, though, it isn't only the physical exertion that triggers such thoughts. More often the problem is in facing a shortage of minutes and hours every day to do the things I'd really like to do or even the things I need to do.

At one point, I drove 125 miles every day to get our children to and from their schools. After-school activities, appointments for doctors, dentists, therapists, and so on, all added to the regular routine. When I was faced with the possibility that I would be part of building a boarding school for kids in crisis, my response was, "The heart is willing, but the body is weak."

Shortly after that Easter night, Bob and some of our friends formed a steering committee. The committee included six families. Most of the people who served on the committee had full-time jobs. The only time they could work on developing their vision for Calvary Academy was during the evenings and on their days off. I was busy taking care of our kids, but I felt like I had to do my share of the work.

We added a phone line in our home to improve our ability to communicate academy business. By default I was given the job of answering the academy phone. After sending two newsletters to a limited number of people, the phone began ringing.

Parents, grandparents, teachers, and pastors called to talk about kids listening to friends instead of their parents, listening to the music of people willing to say anything to sell a tape or CD, imitating the sexual promiscuity portrayed in movies and on TV. They shared their concern that drugs, truancy, and gangs were all too common. Most of these calls ended with a question: When will the academy be open?

My answer then was, I don't know; it's going to take a while.

In return, I would hear a sigh as the caller realized it might not become a reality in time for his or her child. The simple bottom line was that a lot of kids were listening to Satan's worldly messages and following his deceptive will. And a lot of parents were looking for a godly way to help their wayward child.

Every call reinforced the need for such a school. The people involved in developing the project quickly discovered that we each had a limited capacity to do everything that had to be done but that God also provided the skills and special interests and abilities for everyone to play a role in making the dream come true. The apostle Paul described such efforts in this way: "The body is a unit, though it is made up of many parts. . . . In fact God has arranged the parts in the body, every one of them, just as he wanted them to be. If they were all one part, where would the body be? Now you are the body of Christ, and each one of you is a part of it" (1 Corinthians 12:12,18,19,27).

It was obvious that many different talents were needed. What were mine? Thirty years of parenting, many of those with kids having special needs; the ability to find people who could teach me parenting skills for each child's needs; writing (but probably not the type needed); and cooking—a skill already appreciated when the steering committee held meetings over Sunday afternoon dinners. What threw me was when someone said, "Bonnie, you start building a database." My honest response was, "What's a database?" Sometimes the heart is willing, but the brain is weak.

My greatest asset for the committee was that I was willing to work cheap until we had enough money to hire someone who knew what he or she was doing.

Meanwhile, we copied three verses and taped them to the wall over our computer:

"Let us run with perseverance the race marked out for us" (Hebrews 12:1).

"I can do everything through him who gives me strength" (Philippians 4:13).

"Nothing is impossible with God" (Luke 1:37).

In God's time, Calvary Academy opened, thanks to the many willing hearts and the sharing of talents that the Lord brought together to build it. In the overall scheme of things, my part was very small. But it taught me the lesson that even a reluctant worker "can do everything through him who gives [us] strength." Somewhere at the academy there's a database to prove it.

CHAPTER TEN

A Time to Write

Writers call it *writer's block*. It happens when a writer can't seem to get meaningful words from her head through her hands onto paper or a computer screen. I've been "blocked" for almost six weeks now, which for me is an extraordinarily long time not to be writing. I find myself wondering if this might be God's way of telling me to spend more time caring for my family's needs right now.

But my writing time is also embedded somewhere in that passage in Ecclesiastes. You know: A time to do this and a time to do that and . . . *a time to write.*

It's not that writing is always my most enjoyable pastime. Sometimes it's the last thing I want to do. Yet, over the past 30 years, when "the block" comes, even in matters that have nothing to do with writing, my way of handling them has always been to jump in to my least favorite, put-off-the-longest tasks and just do them. And it has usually worked.

This means that the laundry in the laundry room that was beginning to spill out into the family room is once more confined to its designated space. The wallpaper mural, purchased so long ago, is finally hanging on the bathroom wall. The new mini-blinds for Jenna's bedroom are in place. Of course, that leaves a few things like painting Jenna's bedroom and the downstairs hallway that's been taped for a year now, waiting for paint, and the bathroom, which could also use a little brightening to go along with the mural.

However, I still feel the need to write.

Perhaps it's time to consider why this is.

Writing is a form of personal therapy. It's a way to sort through my feelings about things happening around me. The happy times I want to remember. The frustrating times I want to understand. The things I can't control. How often I've handed the Lord such problems through my writing! The year, for example, that getting ready for Christmas was overwhelming; I wrote about it. I complained to God that there didn't even seem to be enough time to bake Christmas cookies. I didn't like the feeling of being overwhelmed. I asked him to change my attitude.

The next day an equally busy neighbor appeared with a platter of homemade cookies to say thank you to me for running a few errands for her. I took her gift as my answer from God. He was telling me to keep things in perspective. And, thankfully, I didn't feel so overwhelmed after that, which left room in my heart to enjoy Christmas.

Perhaps this is the answer to dealing with writer's block: keep things in perspective. As Paul wrote, "If the willingness is there, the gift is acceptable according to what one has, not according to what he does not have" (2 Corinthians 8:12).

Perhaps I worry too much about what should be written. Perhaps it's a little like the poor widow's gift in Mark 12:42-44. As the parable goes: "A poor widow came and put in two very small copper coins, worth only a fraction of a penny. Calling his disciples to him, Jesus said, 'I tell you the truth, this poor widow has put more into the treasury than all the others. They all gave out of their wealth; but she, out of her poverty, put in everything—all she had to live on.'"

The Lord was pleased with the widow's gift simply because of the intentions of her heart when she gave it. So my job is to ask for a giving heart with the right intentions for every task I do . . . whether it be cooking, dusting, caring for others' needs, solving a crisis . . . or writing an article or a book. It doesn't have to be earthshaking. It's all a matter of keeping things in perspective and remembering that the Lord can do a lot with two insignificant copper coins.

CHAPTER ELEVEN

By Faith, Not by Sight

As a preschooler, I remember being fascinated by my mother's framed print of Jesus walking on the water and reaching out to a sinking Peter. "Peter forgot to walk by faith," my mother would explain.

Then she would add the words that Jesus said as he chided Peter: "You of little faith . . . why did you doubt?" (Matthew 14:31) or Paul's words in 2 Corinthians, "We live by faith, not by sight" (5:7). Soon I was repeating these texts right along with her.

That was how I grew up, knowing the words and believing them in my heart. Yet when my husband and I were deciding whether or not to adopt another child, one with special needs, these words about faith were easily forgotten.

Being the parent of a child with special needs can be hard. Satan loves to lay the seeds of doubt: "Are you sure you can handle this?" As Peter discovered, forgetting to reach out to Jesus usually means you're about to sink.

Our children's files include terms like *oppositional behavior, abused, neglected, diabetic, dyslexic, attention deficit, hyperactive, seizures, attachment disorder, fetal alcohol effect, emotional difficulties, poor impulse control, psychotic,* and *post-traumatic stress disorder.* Many years ago, when we began adopting, these words weren't even part of my vocabulary. Sometimes on a "sinking" day, I find myself wishing they still weren't. On really difficult days (the kind that finds my house a disaster, the laundry room full of laundry and none of it's clean, and the school calling to say, "Come and get your son because he's having a rough day"), my only consolation is in knowing that at no time have all these terms ever applied to just one child. I have a plaque on one of our kitchen walls that says what I need to be reminded of on such days. It says, "It's God's work; today he's using me to do it." Our time here on earth is only for a little while, and right now the Lord has work for us to do. We do it to his glory.

On the way to school to pick up our wayward son, I had some prayer time. I asked Jesus to send his love through me. I want my fearful child, who is expecting to face an angry mom, to be able to sense love in my voice when I say something like "Rough day, huh?"

We console ourselves by thinking that progress is being made when there are fewer summons to school each year for the same child. Amazingly, the number of incidents, intensity of incidents, and frequency of incidents with each child do decrease. Having a family that is consistent and loving plays a big role in such incremental progress.

Our children can't be cured of the special needs that they had when they came into our family. The traumas they were exposed to before they came can't be erased. We do what we can with what we have. And what we have is God's Word. So we share it with them.

A favorite passage is Romans 8:28: "We know that in all things God works for the good of those who love him, who have been called according to his purpose."

Telling our kids about Peter and how Jesus is always ready to reach out to them too when they start to sink is a great beginning. My prayer is that someday, instead of chiding them with "You of little faith . . . why did you doubt?" Jesus may say to each of my children, "Well done, good and faithful servant!" (Matthew 25:21).

Even on the rough days, I can thank Jesus for allowing me to be a part of my children's lives. In difficult times God can, and does, work for our good.

CHAPTER TWELVE

The Dirty Thumbnail

It's a typical Sunday morning in the Wasser household.

Nick can't find a matching pair of socks. So, okay, let him wear two blue ones with different stripes on top. But tell him to keep his pant legs down!

The bad smell in the kitchen is getting worse! A quick check reveals: "Josh, you forgot to take out the trash last night. When we have fresh fish, don't wait until the wastebasket is full. You have to get fish remains out immediately. . . . Yes, I see you're ready for church, but if you don't get the wastebasket out now, we'll have to move out of the house when we get back from church. Just be careful of your good clothes. And turn the exhaust fan on."

"What do you mean you're supposed to sing in second service today? Why didn't you tell us last night? We could have slept in another hour. . . . No, I don't mean you should go back to bed. We're almost ready now, and we're going to the early service. You can also attend the second service, and we'll send someone back to pick you up. . . . Yes, I promise I won't forget like last time."

Finally all ten of us are in the van and on our way. I have a few minutes to pull my thoughts together and get ready to worship. Oh, dear, I forgot to get something up from the freezer to thaw for dinner. Well, as Bob would say, that's what a microwave is for. So—what are we going to have for dinner?

Twenty minutes later, I've mentally searched our huge freezer, reviewed the past week's dinners, and decided to have chicken tonight. As we pull into the parking lot at church, I congratulate myself on avoiding another meal crisis.

Moments later, as we walk into church, I remind myself to keep my mind from wandering this week, unlike last week when . . . Oh, now I remember, I said some individuals could no longer sit next to each other because they giggled and fidgeted and talked during the sermon. But to which two had I said that? Well, if I can't remember, I won't worry about it. Maybe they'll remember on their own.

The organ is playing softly. It's time for the opening hymn. On the altar is the Communion ware; I feel a great need to commune with my Lord today. As we finish the hymn and begin the liturgy, I realize that I'll have to concentrate during confession because I haven't prepared very well so far. "Holy and merciful Father, I confess that I am by nature sinful and that I have disobeyed you in my thoughts, words, and . . ."

Oh, what is Megan doing over there? Ah, now I remember! She's one of the two who were supposed to sit next to me this week because they wouldn't be quiet during the sermon last week. Too late now. I don't want to make a scene and distract others as they prepare.

Now, where was I? I guess I missed my confession time, so I'd better do this on my own, even if the sermon has already started.

As usual, I have a long list, Lord. To begin with I've been procrastinating on making dinner lately because I've been trying to get other things done. The bad thing is that then I get upset when everyone is ready to eat and dinner isn't. I've even yelled at the kids because they were hungry. I'm afraid I'm not being a very good mother, am I.

Lord, remind me of this when someone says what a great job I'm doing raising all these kids. You and I know my struggle. Help me find a humble reply and teach me to put my pride aside.

Speaking of mothers, I wonder how mine is feeling? I've been so busy that I've put her needs at the bottom of my priorities. Yet, like you, Lord, she's never put me on the bottom of her list.

Oh, I forgot to send that card to my neighbor after she had surgery. It's sitting on the window sill. She has so little family left, I really should have . . .

Lord, there are a lot of other things too. I was impatient with Josh when he didn't set the table for the right number of people last night. But I know how difficult that is with our teenagers coming and going. I growled at Tara when she wanted help with her social studies. I was less than enthusiastic when making Bob dinner at 10:00 P.M. when he finally got home from work—after leaving at 7:00 that morning. He was in a great mood; I was, well, cranky.

A glance at my watch says the sermon is half over so I'd better try a more generalized approach if I want to be ready before Communion begins.

Let's see: Lack of consideration for others. (I should have let that lady go ahead of me with her half-full shopping cart at the supermarket instead of making her wait for my heaping cart to be checked out.) Reluctance to walk by faith. (Maybe the two-year-old boy offered by social services was meant to be our son. Why did I close the door so fast just because two-year-olds are not my favorite age to parent?) Lack of good judgment, caring, trying . . .

As everyone stands, I realize the pastor has finished preaching. Time's a wastin'.

Lord, I'm not always fair. I don't give of myself if it's really inconvenient. I think nasty thoughts about other people. I don't always put the best construction on things that other people do . . . especially my kids. And I don't spend enough time studying your Word, Lord. Best example, I just missed another sermon opportunity.

But, Lord, I have probably covered most of my immediate sins. I really want to do better. Please let me approach your table, Lord. Forgive me and help me to stop doing all these things.

As the words of institution echo through the church, I'm in awe. "Our Lord Jesus Christ, on the night he was betrayed, took bread; and when he had given thanks, he broke it and gave it to his disciples, saying, 'Take and eat; this is my body, which is given for you. Do this in remembrance of me.'

"Then he took the cup, gave thanks, and gave it to them, saying, 'Drink from it, all of you; this is my blood of the new covenant, which is poured out for you for the forgiveness of sins. Do this, whenever you drink it, in remembrance of me.'"

The Lord Jesus spoke those words for me, I remind myself as I approach the altar. As I kneel at the Lord's Table, I think, *This time I am prepared to be here.* Folding my hands, I bow my head . . . and catch my breath. There on the thumb of my right hand, under the nail, is a black mark. I washed my hands this morning just before we left for church—to make sure I'd gotten the fish smell off. Yet, how many smudges of sin did I encounter between home and here? between the pew and this altar? And was I being prideful in thinking I could ever be totally prepared?

Humbly, I realize there is always a smudge somewhere. Like Paul, I can say, "I know that nothing good lives in me, that is, in my sinful nature. For I have the desire to do what is good, but I cannot carry it out. For what I do is not the good I want to do; no, the evil I do not want to do—this I keep on doing" (Romans 7:18,19).

As I share in his Communion, I pray, "Here I am again, Lord, with my dirty thumbnail and my sinful life. Forgive me. And strengthen me, for Jesus' sake. Amen."

And then, like a huge gong clanging in my head, I hear those words again in my memory: "given" and "poured out for you for the forgiveness of sins." And I am relieved to know once again that I am clean from head to toe in the presence of my heavenly Father because Jesus has washed me.

CHAPTER THIRTEEN

A Stinky Problem

It always amazes me how things can be so good one day and the next day something happens that leads me to wonder why I ever thought I could make it as a mother. Maybe the real question is this: How does one go about resigning?

What happened, you ask?

Well, this is really all about a rather stinky problem. Only two of our four garbage cans were taken out for pickup today. The other two are still in their little "house." Full.

To some this would hardly seem like a justifiable reason to withdraw from motherhood. However, one must realize that the two cans still left in their little house are the two that have remnants of fresh fish . . . well, decomposing fish. It gets worse. Every child in the house has officially declared that it isn't his or her fault. Each has an excuse. Or so it would seem.

Some of the older ones said, "We took our two cans down, and that was our share."

One daughter overslept, claiming, "My sister kept talking all night long, and I couldn't get to sleep. So I was tired."

The youngest son waited for everybody else because he can't carry a full can by himself, and when no one came, he came back inside and left the cans outside.

Others said they saw their youngest brother coming back inside and figured all the cans were already down. No, they didn't bother to ask. Nor did they go out and check. They just assumed.

This means everyone has an excuse, and our family is going to have too much garbage to fit into the garbage cans during the coming week. And we dare not leave the garbage outside in trash bags because of our cute "friends," the raccoons. So now what? This doesn't qualify as a real catastrophe, does it? No, I'll admit it isn't a bonafide catastrophe; but I'm still upset.

I'll admit to having had my share of experience with getting upset. Over the years I've learned that the best way to handle the upsetting moments in life is to reach for God's Word.

Like my daughter who claimed she overslept because her sister talked too much, there are those in the Bible who, like Adam, used excuses and pointed fingers to justify their own wrongdoing. "The woman you put here with me—she gave me some fruit from the tree, and I ate it" (Genesis 3:12).

And then Eve: "The serpent deceived me, and I ate" (verse 13).

Then there are examples of people who, like my son, said they weren't strong enough or good enough or able to talk well enough. Hear Moses telling the Lord: "O Lord, I have never been eloquent, neither in the past nor since you have spoken to your servant. I am slow of speech and tongue" (Exodus 4:10).

Excuses, excuses.

Over and over we read "not my fault, God." This happens especially when we're asked to do something for him and don't follow through.

It seems my children are just following their human nature. And adults aren't much better. I wonder how many excuses I've given the Lord lately.

Fortunately, the Lord doesn't make excuses. He took pity on us and then took action that reflected his grace and mercy. He sent Jesus into our world of sin to fulfill the law when we could not. He took action: Christ died for us. There's the example for all of us to follow. No excuses; just do it and get the job done. Rather than getting bogged down in excuses, just remember the words of Colossians 3:23, "Whatever you do, work at it with all your heart, as working for the Lord, not for men."

Working for the Lord with all my heart in whatever I do will be my example for others. That means overlooking the excuses and concentrating on finding solutions to the problems.

As for today's problem, maybe this is the time to let natural consequences teach the stinky pitfalls of making excuses and the benefits of taking responsibility.

It would probably also be a good time to look for better ways to recycle.

CHAPTER FOURTEEN

Somewhere a Grandma Is Praying

"Why have you adopted so many kids?"

"How can you parent all those kids?"

These are questions we hear often. The *why* is a question for which I have yet to find an adequate answer. For the *how*, the short answer probably is "We do it by prayer." A good example would be the story of our son who came to our family for a weekend of respite when he was eight and a half . . . and stayed until he was eventually adopted.

When he came, we didn't know he'd been abused as part of a loosely organized group that some individuals labeled a cult. We did know we had a charming, sometimes loving, sometimes out-of-control little boy who now was our son. We also knew that he embraced our Christian faith because he'd had a grandma who took him to church. When his father terminated his parental rights, Grandma told our son that because she lived so close to his dad, she could no longer bring him to her house. She reassured him that God would find him a family. She promised to pray for him and his family every day.

Prior to coming into our home, our son blew through three foster or adoptive homes in six months. After he came, we quickly found we needed those prayers his grandmother had promised and then some. We also discovered that we needed strong arms to wrap around him and hold him tight when he was physically out of control. And when we failed to keep him under control, it meant that he would trash our home. Sometimes we had to hold him for an hour or even two before he was calm enough to talk. Initially we had no idea why his behaviors varied so radically. Nor were we aware that he was afraid to tell us.

Three weeks after he came, an older brother caught him playing with matches in his bedroom. Before I could get upstairs, he ran downstairs, out a back door, into the woods, and out of sight. Several kids walked the woods but saw no sign of him.

Less than an hour later, as I was looking up the non-emergency number for the police, our phone rang. It was our social worker calling from a city 60 miles away. She asked if we were missing a little boy. To my reply of "How did he get to you so fast?" she laughed and said she'd gotten a call from a social worker in our son's home county (four hours away from us) after they had gotten a call from the police department in our town.

I quickly placed my call to the chief of police, who promised to return our son to our home right away. He explained our son had met some construction workers on the other side of the woods, told them he'd been squirrel hunting with his father, became frightened when his drunken father began waving his gun around, and ran away. He said he had stayed in the woods overnight and was lost and was hungry. The construction workers bought him lunch at a local deli and then dropped him off at the police station on their way back to work. This was to be one of the lighter, more creative encounters between the police and this little boy, but it certainly wasn't the last.

During the next two years, we managed to survive the storms, although there were days when I was quite certain one of us was not going to. Our son's pattern of running to avoid consequences continued. We intensified his therapy sessions and increased their number to weekly, even after he'd disclosed past abuses in his birth family. In fact, after he began disclosing, we saw a more anxious child than we'd had before. The normal reaction for most kids would be to relax after sharing a horrible secret. On the other hand, the abuses he was disclosing were some of the worst I had ever heard. And having worked with a lot of troubled children, I had heard a lot. Still, he did nothing to ratchet up our concern until the day he ran away and started two fires in the community.

Thankfully, property damage was minimal and no one was injured. But that episode was a very clear indication that our son needed more help than we could give him at home. We hospitalized him and prayed for the best.

Two months later, after multiple tests and countless hours of therapy, we brought our son back home, definitely not healed, but at least more willing to talk.

The next week we returned to our regular therapist. There, with uncharacteristic calm, this troubled son of ours disclosed even more past abuses. Then, while the therapist and I were scheduling the next week's appointment, he disappeared for about two minutes. When he calmly returned, he gave me a hug. I thought little of it at the time. I was wondering instead about a remark he made every time we drove home. He would always say, "At least I didn't fall apart today."

As in the past, I assured him that crying—or falling apart—wasn't wrong. "It's okay to cry." He never seemed convinced. And I felt as though I was missing something important—something that should have been obvious.

At home, I ran my answering machine and found an urgent message from the therapist. During those two minutes our son was out of my sight, he had trashed five therapists' offices at the clinic. He poured coffee and water over papers; swept papers, pencils, and books onto the floor; and overturned chairs. This was a large clinic. Thankfully, some therapists were in their offices because he had trashed every office not in use at the time.

Therapy sessions, hospitalizations, and finding alternative school settings where he might feel safe and at least learn became a routine way of handling things over the next several years. Eventually we learned that his fear of "falling apart" after he made disclosures in a therapy session occurred because he believed what his abusers in the cult had told him. They had told him that they had planted a bomb inside him. If he ever revealed what had been done to him or told anyone about their Satanic worship, the bomb would go off, blowing him and everyone around him to smithereens.

Our son continued to hallucinate, but eventually he began to realize that as real as these experiences seemed to him, no one else could see the things he was seeing. That meant they weren't actually happening. These hallucinatory episodes were a little like bad nightmares that would happen while he was awake. As the years passed, he learned to trust us. He began to believe us when we told him that the things he was seeing weren't really there. Then he began to learn techniques that would help him check the hallucinations by himself.

Sometimes he panicked and threatened violence because he had confused us with his abusers. His abusers had probably given him drugs and alcohol before and during the abuses. If these had included hallucinatory drugs, it might explain his ongoing pattern of not being sure about what was real and what wasn't.

A few times he even picked up a weapon and tried to use it. We always managed to disarm him before he would hurt someone. Then we would take him back to the hospital.

The few of our friends who had occasionally provided respite care for some of our children when Bob and I wanted to get away asked us not to bring this child back for more care. He was more than they could handle. We struggled on, often reminding our son, and ourselves, that somewhere his grandma was praying for him.

With each hospitalization someone on the staff would ask, "Are you sure you want to take him home again?" or "Is this the time to start looking for a long-term residential facility for him?" Each time we prayed and pondered. Each time we asked God to help us find a way to continue to live safely with him at home, to keep the other kids' lives on an even keel while we did what we could to help him, and to maintain our own sanity at the same time. Amazingly, each time the Lord found a way.

Today our son has been with us longer than he lived with his birth father. He seldom confuses us with the people who hurt him. His trust is far greater than it once was. He's decided that he wants to be our son, no matter what he has to do to make it work. And he is trying.

The challenges continue. We're all realistic about the probability that he will need to go back for occasional hospital stays. We're also aware that the day may come when it won't be safe to have him continue living at home. Meanwhile we pray and work for his healing . . . and rejoice when we see it.

Would you call this a miracle? I suppose it could be called that. Are we surprised? Not really. Somewhere a grandma is praying. I pray for her too. Someday I hope to tell her thank you.

There is no doubt that God hears our prayers. The Bible says that "he answered their prayers, because they trusted in him" (1 Chronicles 5:20). At this time, God's answer to his grandma's prayers, and ours, is to keep our son living at home with us.

CHAPTER FIFTEEN

Take This Cup from Me . . .

He lunged at me with the long barbecue fork—trying to stab me—trying to kill me. It was going to be one of the bad days trying to live with our son, then age 12.

Bob and I took him back to the psychiatric hospital that afternoon. During the hour-long drive, he alternated between vulgar and hateful and detached and uncaring (the latter was a relief from the former). It was a difficult thing to bear. Here was a little boy afraid that he'd done something so bad this time that we'd never bring him home again.

I was on my own roller coaster of emotions, which vacillated from wanting to wrap him in my love and heal him to leaving him in the doctor's care so that I would never have to cope with his psychotic behaviors again. And I questioned: "How long, Lord? How long can I go on?"

It would be our son's seventh hospital admission in two years. The 24-month behavior pattern before that ranged from unpredictable to bizarre to charming. His mischief included setting fires, stealing, running away, and a few less serious episodes, like putting small stones in the gas tanks of our cars and leaving obscene messages on school tape recorders. At least we knew why he did these things. He experienced nightmares almost every night. Before he came to us at age 8, he had been terribly abused and he had witnessed horrible things.

Had we known how hurt he was, would we have adopted him? I don't know. Perhaps the Lord in his wisdom hadn't told us this for a very good reason. So the question continued to nag: "Lord, how long can I go on?" And that particular evening Jesus' words in the Garden of Gethsemane kept echoing through my thoughts: "Father, if you are willing, take this cup from me" (Luke 22:42).

Was I asking God to take my son from me? Yes. At that moment, I truly was.

Yet, how many times had I also considered the rest of Jesus' prayer: "Yet not my will, but yours be done." I guess I'd have to admit that on that night I was not interested in remembering those words.

The Lord had given this struggling young man to me. I was—I am—his mother. Yet, being willing to be his mother wasn't enough. The strength for being his mother seemed to be gone. Saint Luke goes on to report that "an angel . . . appeared to [Jesus] and strengthened him. And being in anguish, he prayed more earnestly" (verses 43,44).

I prayed more earnestly. I knew instinctively that I needed more of God's strength. I knew this because the Bible tells me that "I can do everything through him who gives me strength" (Philippians 4:13). That was the only way we could get through this and still be able to make a difference in his young life.

A week later Bob and I returned to the hospital. The doctors described our son's violence and anger toward me as "misplaced anger." (I was glad he missed my body with the barbecue fork too.) They felt he was striking out at the birth mother who'd hurt him. The year before, our son had worked through similar emotions with his birth father and adoptive father. Now it was my turn.

How violent would he become? No one would even venture a guess. Was I in physical danger? Probably. How much? No one could say.

The decision was ours to make. Did we want to take him home again?

I struggled as I considered the question. Bob waited for an answer to come from me. The danger was mine. I thought again, "I can do everything through him who gives me strength." Would I be able to remember that thought when I really needed to remember it?

Slowly, I nodded my head. "We want to take him home as soon as we can."

Six weeks later, after an evaluation of his medication regime and with some added intense therapy, we took our son home.

Some days it almost felt as though we were a normal family again. But there were other days when I wondered if we would make it through the next hour. The doctors hinted that he'd eventually have to go back to the hospital again.

Finally, after eight months at home—the longest continuous time he'd spent with us in the past two and a half years—that day arrived. The violence this time around had been minimal; the issues, quickly identified; and in three weeks, our son was home again with his family.

Three months later we readmitted him again for acting-out behaviors in school. But none of this behavior was violent. He spent the next several weeks sorting through these new issues before coming home to his family again. Since then there have been only two short hospital stays of two weeks one time and four days the last. None included violence. They dealt instead with his own fear that he might become violent again some time in the future.

Today, with a carefully monitored medication routine and a structured behavior-modification program, he's doing the best he's ever done. He may need a hospital setting for a while someday again. But at least that possibility doesn't look so ominous right now.

There are times when I actually forget how hard it was— how hard it can be. We still live one day at a time. We're constantly looking for new ways to help our son heal and become a whole person. We tell him and show him that we love him. We tell him that God loves him too. We do that a lot. And each night I pray, "Remember us tomorrow, Lord. And thank you for today. Thank you for one more day."

CHAPTER SIXTEEN

As We Forgive . . .

Forgive us our sins, as we forgive . . .

For years I've been trying to misinterpret that part of the Lord's Prayer. There are so many other ways the Lord could have put it. He could have said, "Forgive us our trespasses because we know we've done wrong." Or, "Forgive us because we're sorry and will try hard never, ever to do it again." God didn't. Instead, Jesus told his followers to pray, "Forgive us . . . as we forgive others."

My record on this score isn't always the one I'd like to see my children imitate. It's not that I don't want to forgive. It's just that it's so hard sometimes. For example, I had a tough time forgiving when my emotionally delayed 18-year-old daughter's "friends" kept telling her she didn't have to listen to her parents anymore. Never mind that she was about 14 in her maturity level. Her birth certificate and her friends claimed she was legally an adult! By the time we were able to convince her that we really had only her best interests in mind, she was 19. And by then, in my exhaustion, I had forgotten about dealing with my anger and forgiving her friends. Now I can't even remember their names.

There have been other times when forgiving didn't even feel like an option. It was difficult to even consider forgiving the person who date raped another daughter. The honest truth is that it felt good to see him convicted. Afterward I simply wanted to use my energy to help our daughter deal with her feelings of depression and anxiety and her hesitation to trust her own judgment in relationships again. Justice had been served. But forgive him? Let's just say it was my hope never to see him again and leave it at that.

It has also been hard for me to forgive the people who hurt my children before they came to our family. How does one go about forgiving men who have satisfied their own sexual appetites with a seven-year-old's body? How does one forgive parents who "forgot" to feed their baby because going to a bar and getting drunk was their only goal in life?

Then there's the more immediate problem of forgiving one son who can't seem to stop taking things that don't belong to him. Each time we catch him, he promises never to do it again. How many times do we forgive him?

Yet Jesus taught us to pray, "Forgive us our sins, as we forgive those who sin against us."

It isn't easy. The apostle Paul encouraged, " 'In your anger do not sin': Do not let the sun go down while you are still angry, and do not give the devil a foothold" (Ephesians 4:26,27).

Do not give the devil a foothold . . . in my heart? in my life?

Proverbs 28:14 adds, "Blessed is the man who always fears the LORD, but he who hardens his heart falls into trouble."

Are we hardening our hearts when we fail to forgive others? when we don't make the time to forgive? when we don't want to forgive? Is it possible that this is why there's a correlation between the Lord's forgiving us as we forgive others? Is it possible that putting it this way in his model prayer was the way Christ chose to keep before us that little word *as,* so we won't have the chance to forget . . . and give the devil his foothold?

When forgiving others is difficult, it helps to remember the words Christ spoke while suspended on a cross: "Forgive them, for they do not know what they are doing" (Luke 23:34). There's the real model for forgiveness.

CHAPTER SEVENTEEN

A Time to Live

A decision every adopted child must make some time in life is whether or not to search for a personal history and his or her birth parents. It can be a frightening time, especially for kids who were removed from their birth family by the courts. Often these children, usually labeled as children having "special needs," tend to remember one or both birth parents with mixed feelings. They feel love because there is a natural connection with their birth parents, but they also fear their parents, who might hurt them again. The media portray adoptee-parent reunions as wonderful things—everyone lives happily ever after. But the media seldom stick around long enough to uncover the whole story.

As parents of 20 now-adult adoptees, we have always supported our children if they wanted to search for their birth families. We've learned that a reunion may shake our son's or daughter's relationship with us for the moment, but eventually our relationships are strengthened as the result of such a search.

No two of these reunions have been alike, though all were good in the beginning. Our most disappointing experience with reunions occurred when our son Scott was reunited with his birth mother, Patti.

After all the difficulties Scott had during his growing-up years, things were looking a little better by the time he was in his 20s. He was in counseling, attempting to understand his past mistakes so they wouldn't be repeated. He was taking medication, and he was working. Yet he said he felt there was something missing in his life.

His therapist suggested that he begin searching for his birth mother. The therapist said it might help Scott fill in some of the missing pieces to the puzzle that was his life.

Scott had no memory of Patti. The courts had terminated her parental rights on the basis of child neglect during Scott's second year of life. He was curious enough to wade through the state's recommended search procedure to find her. We took this as a sign of his increasing maturity.

They met first on paper, sharing information through the state search program.

Next they talked by phone.

Finally, they both felt comfortable with the idea of meeting each other, so the arrangements were made.

When we saw them together for the first time, there could be no doubt that the two were mother and son. Scott believed she was the answer to his prayers. The rest of us hoped he was right.

At Patti's insistence, and in spite of our reservations, Scott quit his job and moved to her hometown several hours away. She argued that they could get to know each other better and make up for the lost years. The rest of us increased our prayers as we saw Scott leave with high hopes.

The ecstasy lasted less than a week.

He received a cool reception from his birth brother and sister, which made him uncomfortable. In one of his many phone calls, he said that the more he got to know them, the less he wanted to be around them. Scott had made some big mistakes in his life, even committing felonies. But these two topped everything he had done.

His sister was pregnant, unmarried, and using drugs with the baby's father. She was furious when Scott tried to tell her how the drugs might affect her baby.

His brother not only used drugs but, at 17, also sold them. He was also running from the law because he was wanted for armed robbery.

As for Patti, well, she wasn't interested in talking about why she had given Scott up for adoption. She insisted that none of it was her fault. According to her telling of the story, the social workers had taken Scott away from her.

Scott persisted in getting an answer to his primary question: "Why did you let them?"

Finally, one day Patti glared at him as she nervously paced the living room floor. "They said I wasn't taking care of you. I don't know why they said that. I fed you. They claimed I left you alone. But I never left until you were asleep, and I was never gone long. I had a right to have some fun too while your father was having his fun. It wasn't my fault, Scott. It wasn't!" She challenged him to contradict her.

Hearing that made Scott feel as though someone had slammed his head into a brick wall. He was furious; he wanted to punch someone—something—the way he'd punched the wall while growing up.

He left Patti's building. He feared he might hit his mother if he went back to her apartment. He couldn't remember feeling this angry before. Still, he had managed to hold it together.

While Scott had legally taken his adoptive family's name, Patti insisted on calling him by his birth name: Scott Timothy Wilson. He became confused about his identity. He wondered why he had been so eager to search for his birth family. And he wanted to know why the social workers had taken him away from Patti.

Social services had permitted Scott to see part of his file when he began the search. He had learned a lot about the earliest part of his life. The record said he had been found alone in their apartment, crying, lying in a box, surrounded by bottles—some with curdled milk in them. He screamed when they tried to pick him up, so they carried him to the hospital in his box. He was dirty. A bad diaper rash required medical attention. He was not able to eat solid foods.

At first they thought he might be mentally retarded; he could neither talk nor walk. The court had concluded that his birth mother had not been ready to be a full-time mother.

Yet, nothing in Scott's history could account for the anger he had felt in the years that followed. He threw tantrums, lied, stole precious things from his foster families, ran away, and got into fights. Oh, how he had tried to change! But he always blew it by losing his temper.

There had been some good times. His foster family was really neat. But they never adopted him. They feared that they would be unable to care for him as he got into his teens. They wanted him to have a family that could. Scott couldn't get them to change their minds.

Then, when Scott was in the fifth grade, we adopted him. Everyone tried to reassure him, telling him that this family had experience raising kids. He wasn't so sure. And the unexplained rage kept gnawing away inside.

When Scott was 16, a different psychologist gave the rage a name: *reactive attachment disorder.* Because he had been neglected during his first year of life, Scott had never learned to trust people in the way that normal babies are supposed to trust. If he was hungry, he couldn't trust anyone to feed him. If he was wet, he had no one to trust to make him comfortable again. If he was scared, he had no adults to reassure him the way most babies have.

Trust is not a small matter. And the way Scott came to understand how the world worked had made him his own worst enemy. Whenever he started to rely on someone, he would test that person until he or she finally failed. Would things have been different if his birth mother had given him up sooner? Maybe. But she hadn't; now he had to find a way to live with it and work things out.

His search had started with great hope and anticipation. Now, thinking about going back to Patti's, he saw the whole thing as a disaster. Patti obviously didn't want him asking questions. Instead, he reminded her of a part of her personal history she preferred to forget.

Scott called home. We were there on the other end, on two extensions. We guessed that Patti perhaps felt guilty about neglecting him. We encouraged Scott to go back and reassure her by telling her that he had forgiven her. Maybe then they would again be able to talk about substantive matters.

He followed our advice, but things didn't improve. So he asked us for money and bought a bus ticket home. With our help and encouragement, he got an apartment, went back to counseling, and began taking medication once again for depression.

We walked together and talked frequently with Scott after his return. We reminded him that Patti could have chosen abortion instead of life for him and that he could feel grateful for the fact that she had not. But that caused even more anxiety for Scott. Instead of being thankful for the gift of life, he found himself wondering if it would have been better if Patti had aborted him. He saw his life as more of a burden to others than a gift from God. As for the other people in his life, his foster family had moved to another part of the country and he now believed they had forgotten him. Patti certainly didn't want him in her life.

One night he decided to do what Patti hadn't done—bring an end to his life to finally take the hurt away. So Scott swallowed all of the pills that remained in his prescription, washing them down with alcohol.

When Scott awoke, there were tubes leading from his body into machines, and he realized he was lying in a hospital bed. "Good morning," said a woman whose tag identified her as a nurse. "I'm Kathy. You probably have some questions."

"Yeah. How did I get here?"

"You were brought in about, oh, 3:00 this morning. Unconscious. I'll let the doctor explain the treatment you were given. Looks like you're feeling better."

"Yeah," muttered Scott, turning his head away. She didn't have to tell him any more. He remembered. He'd tried to get rid of all his bad feelings last night, but he thought, *I couldn't even do that right.*

We went to visit him later that day.

"How'd you know I was here?" he asked.

"Your probation officer called us," explained his father.

"I blew it again, didn't I?" mumbled Scott.

Neither of us responded. He saw the tears filling our eyes. I finally gathered my composure enough to say, "No, Scott, you *almost* blew it. But the Lord still has plans for you here on earth."

"Like what?" demanded Scott. He struggled against the hopeful feeling that crept into his heart.

"I guess that's for you to decide," his dad choked. "We're just thankful you have the chance."

The rest of the visit was spent on small talk, catching up on family news. Yet it was as though the three of us knew that Scott had finally reached a turning point. He found himself repeating a favorite Bible verse from Romans chapter 8. "We know that in all things God works for the good of those who love him" (verse 28). Whatever came next wasn't going to be easy. The struggle might even take the rest of his life. But now he believed that God had a purpose for him. We believed the same.

From then on, the most difficult part of Scott's ordeal was thinking about his birth mother, wondering why she hadn't loved him enough to let him go at birth, before he'd gotten hurt and before his ability to trust was destroyed. If she had loved him as she said, why was she telling him to stay out of her life? He even tried once more to make contact with her, but her phone number had been disconnected. Then he tried to write. The letter came back, indicating she had moved with no forwarding address.

Scott has learned to forgive Patti and accepted the fact that she has no place for him in her life. He is thankful she didn't choose abortion. On bad days he buries himself in his art. After the overdose, he began using his art to calm himself. Some of his best work is done during these personal therapy times. When we admire the work, he reminds us that this too was one of the good things spoken of in that text in Romans.

We're all very proud of him. All the members of the Wasser family figure we will be able to say we knew him before he became recognized by the world as a renowned artist.

CHAPTER EIGHTEEN

With Great Patience

Being a mother of so many kids means that people are a little more patient with me when I do something like forgetting to bring my dozen cookies to the school open house. They just figure it goes with the territory. After all, how together can a mother of 25 kids really be?

There are days when I ask myself that same question. For example, when something is missing, I have to stop and search my memory before blaming one of my kids, just in case I'm the one responsible for moving it, taking it, or failing to put it in the right place to begin with. One of our sons, adopted at almost nine years old, made this especially hard for me.

This young man is very bright, has a great sense of humor, and really was a wonderful match for our family—with one exception. He couldn't seem to keep his hands off other people's things. Among the loot we've caught him with are electronic gadgets, nice pens, bags of chocolate chips, Bob's tools, and my change and dollar bills when my purse was left unguarded for even the shortest span of time.

We tried using God's Word to impress on him that stealing is wrong. It is in one of God's commandments; we are not permitted to steal things that don't belong to us. We explained that he was hurting other people when he took their possessions. And, yes, the quarters, dimes, nickels, and dollar bills in my purse are my possessions. We had him write God's commandment "Do not steal" and the Bible verse "No one can serve two masters. Either he will hate the one and love the other, or he will be devoted to the one and despise the other. You cannot serve both God and Money" (Matthew 6:24). We gave him extra chores to earn the money he thought he needed. We explained what the money in my purse was meant for—his needs and the needs of the rest of our family—so he wasn't only hurting me but also his father and brothers and sisters. We prayed for him, we prayed with him, and we encouraged him to pray on his own. We even tried sewing the pockets on his jeans shut. Still, our son couldn't seem to keep his fingers off the things that belonged to other people.

He continued to take stuff that wasn't his to take. When we asked why, his standard answer was, "I saw it there and wanted it."

The years went by with us asking ourselves on a regular basis: "Will we ever get it across to him that stealing is wrong? Will we ever get him to understand that the crummy feelings he has about himself will stay crummy if he continues to steal? Will we ever be able to instill in him a desire to serve God, not money?"

One day, after reading the Bible verse that admonishes Christian adults to let the little children come to Jesus and not to hinder them, I found myself wondering what Jesus would have done if one of those children had stolen stuff from the disciples.

How are we to teach these little ones? Paul told Timothy to use God's Word to "correct, rebuke and encourage—with great patience and careful instruction" (2 Timothy 4:2). That's how we are to help them as they struggle with these temptations in life: *with great patience and careful instruction*. Rather than wondering how long we should keep trying before we give up, it would be better for each of us to consider how the Lord corrects, rebukes, and encourages us. He does so always *with great patience and careful instruction*. The example he gives us is useful and practical.

Our son's weakness is another opportunity for an imperfect mother to share God's grace and everlasting love. With God's help, I'll remind myself to correct, rebuke, and encourage using God's Word. And I'll do it as often and as long as it is necessary.

CHAPTER NINETEEN

The Lord Prepares Us

"I don't think I'm ready for this, Lord."

How many times during my life has the Lord heard me say this? I say it often. And I say it in regard to a lot of different situations that I face in life. With every opportunity to speak to a group and tell our story. Whenever the Lord makes me the mom to a child with special needs. Whenever the chores of ironing, sewing, or cleaning closets loom.

I don't always manage my life well when it comes to preparation. I sure wasn't ready for becoming a parent the first time. Never an admirer of small people as a teenager, I only baby-sat for one of two reasons: I was either desperate for money or my mother insisted. Often the people that I baby-sat for were her personal friends. As she would put it, "You aren't doing anything important anyway." Now, suddenly, we had this tiny child, able to do absolutely nothing on his own. What's worse, everyone expected me to take this helpless baby home. It was probably good that I never felt overconfident. I might have taken my parental responsibilities too lightly had I been so.

I remember praying a lot more than usual after our first son was born. In fact, I've often said that he was raised on prayer. But I guess that could also be said of all of our children. Now that I think of it, maybe that is how God prepared me. I know he gave me loving Christian parents who taught me, by example, to pray often and earnestly. When I became a parent, I already was a natural *pray-er*. As our family grew, it became obvious that I needed to pray my way through each child's childhood.

Being prepared for becoming a parent to a child with special difficulties was an especially tricky matter, particularly when no one, including social workers, anticipated such problems before placing the child. Even then the Lord prepared me in certain ways, though I was unaware of the things he was doing in the background.

Take, for example, the case of the 14-year-old daughter of some friends of our friends. This young woman had begun experimenting with alcohol, was skipping school, and the like. Such adolescent behaviors would be a problem for any teen. For this one, it had the potential to be disastrous because she had insulin-dependent diabetes.

We were asked if she could come and live with our family for a while. Since we knew nothing of the daily care people with diabetes must have, we were reluctant. Her parents assured us she was capable of handling her daily injections and monitoring her blood sugar level. Our job would be to give her support and encouragement.

The young woman had some attitude problems, and she was experiencing growing-up pains; but she was a good teacher in the area of diabetes. Thanks to her expertise, the medical part of her stay went very smoothly.

Several months after she came to stay with us—just long enough for us to get comfortable with dealing with diabetes—we received a call from social services, saying they had two little girls—sisters—who had lost their home. They needed a place to live for a few weeks while the social workers sorted out what was going on. A few weeks later our family doctor diagnosed the younger girl, who was nine years old at the time, with juvenile onset diabetes. She would need daily monitoring and injections. The Lord had prepared us well when he brought the daughter of our friends' friends to live with us. The nine-year-old eventually became our adopted daughter.

Every now and then, I reflect on Ephesians 2:10, which says, "We are God's workmanship, created in Christ Jesus to do good works, which God prepared in advance for us to do." The next time the words "I don't think I'm ready for this, Lord" come out of my mouth, I'll try to remember that God has somehow prepared me in advance for everything he wants me to do. My question? Would ironing, sewing, and cleaning closets be included in his preparations?

Okay, they probably are. But he never said we were going to *enjoy* doing everything he's prepared us to do.

CHAPTER TWENTY

Answers to Prayer

Early in our marriage, my husband shared with me that shortly before we began dating he had been praying for a wife. Over the years I have reminded him of this fact at strategic moments, such as when I've gotten involved in my writing and lost track of the time and dinner's going to be a little late—like two hours. Or when he can't find our only set of car keys and we both know I had them last. Or when I've misread an appointment time and now we're going to be late. "Remember," I would say, "I was the answer to your prayer." It's had the effect of defusing some of the more intense moments in our marriage.

If only all answers to prayers were as clear. While it is quite obvious that the Lord answers prayers, my problem often is in recognizing his answers.

Can this obnoxious 13-year-old, who has been testing our commitment every day for the last six months, really be the answer to our prayer: "Lord, if you want us to adopt another child, find one for us, please"? The next day the phone rang with a call from the state social worker, telling us about a 13-year-old girl who lost her adoptive placement and asking if we have an open bed and room in our family. The worker said they would only consider this a foster placement initially since there was no time for the usual preplacement visits. We could talk about adoption (if it was appropriate) down the road.

Can my impossible-to-balance checkbook really be the answer to the prayer: "Lord, help us find a way to give you our firstfruits"? Maybe I should have omitted that last sentence: "And please don't ever allow us to have so much money that we forget to depend on you."

Can our dream of opening a boarding school for children in crisis really be an answer to "Lord, help me find more time to write"? As things turned out, the building of the school did result in the need to buy a new computer, which allowed me to do much more writing and to do it so much faster than was possible on my old word processor.

Sometimes I get so caught up in wondering if a happening is the Lord's answer to my prayer that I find myself focusing on his answers instead of on my petitions.

Maybe that's a good thing . . . or maybe it isn't. Saint Paul wrote: "Do not be anxious about anything, but in everything, by prayer and petition, with thanksgiving, present your requests to God. And the peace of God, which transcends all understanding, will guard your hearts and your minds in Christ Jesus" (Philippians 4:6,7).

That's an amazing promise. In other words, after presenting my requests to God, my part is to relax and go with the flow rather than to wait anxiously for his reply. Anxiety erases peace. Anxiety is what I must guard against, because anxiety can be symptomatic of not trusting the Lord to answer my prayer in his way for my good. God invites us to put our petitions before him and then trust him to give us his answer, when the time is right and whether the answer is *yes* or *no* or *wait*.

My prayer now is "Lord, don't let me get so caught up in defining your answers that I become anxious at the price of your peace."

Recently, one of our children asked if Bob and I had ever considered getting a divorce. This daughter came from a family where divorce was commonplace. We took her question as a way of probing the stability of her new family. My immediate reply was "No. How could we ever think of such a thing? After all, I was the answer to Dad's prayer." I hope my answer was reassuring. I know I said those words with peace in my heart. And I too gave thanks for our marriage.

CHAPTER TWENTY-ONE

Pharisees among Us

Why did he say those things? There's little truth in them, and the truth that's there is distorted. How does one answer? I want to stand on the rooftop and scream, "Liar! Liar!" I want to stand him before God and man and expose him. Bob says to ignore him and eventually others will too.

How painful it must have been for Jesus when the Pharisees not only refused to recognize him as the Son of God but ridiculed him and tested him, trying to make him look foolish! He doesn't sound happy with them. In Matthew 15:7-9 Jesus quoted Isaiah, saying: "You hypocrites! Isaiah was right when he prophesied about you: 'These people honor me with their lips, but their hearts are far from me. They worship me in vain; their teachings are but rules taught by men.'"

A question occurs to me: Why do some people insist that everything must be looked at their way? Initially, this is probably done with good intentions. Yet one wonders if, in time, stubbornness and self-righteousness creep in until a person begins viewing himself as the ultimate authority. He tells everyone his idea is best because he's well-educated, more knowledgeable, and has been given more authority. He belittles those who suggest an alternative.

Jesus saw this attitude and told the Pharisees, "First clean the inside of the cup and dish, and then the outside also will be clean" (Matthew 23:26). He obviously did not like the know-it-all attitudes of the Pharisees.

So, how does one deal with people who act like the Pharisees? How does one work with an individual who is intent upon doing everything his way, a person who works everything out so that he alone gets the glory and recognition? I'll bet he then stands at the altar and says, "Thank you, God, for giving me such great knowledge and not making me like lesser men"—like the Pharisee's prayer in the parable about the Pharisee and the tax collector.

Thinking about Jesus' parable gives me an uncomfortable feeling. Is my indignation beginning to sound like the Pharisee? It probably would be better to approach this from the angle of the tax collector.

What would the tax collector be saying? "Yes, Lord, I know this guy has it all wrong, but what if he could look into my heart? What if he were to tell others the real truth about me?"

I know one thing, he'd find a lot to say. And he wouldn't have to twist things much to make me look like a sinner. He would know the extent of my impatience at times with my children. He would know how good I am at ignoring or putting off the good deeds I should be doing in the Lord's name. He would know that Sunday after Sunday I find it difficult to remain attentive to the sermon because I keep thinking of things like what I should make for dinner. He would know my self-righteous anger and the nasty thoughts that fill my mind when someone misjudges me or my intentions.

Maybe instead of being indignant with one man, I should be telling the Lord how sorry I am for the actions and thoughts that have been part of my life. Maybe it would be better to say thank you and praise the Lord for allowing a weak and unworthy person like me to contribute to his kingdom's work in even small ways.

Actually, there are no "maybes" about it.

I should forget my indignation over someone else's actions and spend my time and energy on overcoming my weaknesses.

As for my Pharisee, praying for someone who disagrees with me would be a better way of dealing with him than dwelling on the things he says and passing judgment. As Saint

Luke put it, "Bless those who curse you, pray for those who mistreat you" (6:28). Rather than spending time and effort ranting and raving about the Pharisee-like behavior of someone else, it's time to clean the inside of my own cup and dish.

CHAPTER TWENTY-TWO

A Time to Vent

"Men have to think about problems inside their heads. Women need to talk them through." A very wise woman told me that many years ago, during a discussion of how men and women deal differently with their problems. Well, we were facing a problem, and her words were ringing in my ears. Rather than try to get my husband to discuss something before he was ready, I've learned after 40 years of marriage to keep quiet and wait.

But in order to be ready when he finally was, I needed to get my own thoughts together. The only way I knew to go about doing that was to find someone to talk it through with me.

I was searching for someone who could approach things from a position that would not be judgmental—someone who knew me well enough to understand that by venting I could begin to organize my thoughts and become clearer—someone who would listen and not have her own faith undermined by my frustrations—someone who would not feel compelled to offer solutions, because there were no solutions—not at the moment. And not talking things through would simply require too much energy for me to continue to remain silent.

Yes, talking with God was a good avenue to pursue. As always, the Lord was listening. In fact, it was obvious to me that he was saying to wait. And I was willing to wait. I just needed to talk about things while I waited. I needed to share my hurt and confusion with someone who wouldn't be hurt as a result.

Often my writing is a positive direction the Lord gives me in order to vent. This time that wasn't a good approach. In writing I usually look for solutions. In this case it was too soon to be seeking a solution to the unsolvable problem I was confronting.

In my prayers I asked for peace . . . even without acceptance. The only thing I really needed to accept was the fact that God was in charge. My job was to remember: "Do not be anxious about anything, but in everything, by prayer and petition, with thanksgiving, present your requests to God. And the peace of God, which transcends all understanding, will guard your hearts and your minds in Christ Jesus" (Philippians 4:6,7).

The Lord gave me peace. But he did it in a most remarkable way.

My idea was that in sharing my problem with someone else, it would be possible to become a better sounding board for my husband when the time was right.

That night the phone rang. Night calls were always for Bob. I hadn't even considered the possibility that it might be for me. That's why I was so surprised when I realized that Bob was handing me the phone: "It's Char."

Char was a former neighbor, a writer too. "Oh, I left her a message to call me last week," I said. "I figured she had to be out of town because she didn't call back."

Char's first words to my hello were "I'm sorry to bother you at night with everybody home, but first I was out of town and then every time I wanted to call, I couldn't seem to get near the phone because of interruptions on my end. So I decided that tonight—even though I never call you at night—it was finally time to call."

We got caught up on each other's life. I had moved away 24 years ago. Still, over the years we had managed to keep in touch by phone and visits. Sometimes we shared happy news; other times, troubling incidents in our lives. As we talked now, her words "It was finally time to call" kept flashing though my thoughts. Char was a very special person in my life. The best part of our friendship was our mutual walk with the Lord. It was obvious to both of us that the Lord used our friendship to deepen our faith even though we did not belong to the same church or even to the same denomination. Yet, while our practices were different, our personal faiths were based on the Bible truth that we are saved by grace through faith.

I wondered if this call was the answer to my prayer. Was the Lord giving me my chance to vent? I shared a few words about my latest frustration.

Her response was immediate. "Oh, I know what you mean. Except sometimes I hesitate to talk about it."

Our conversation slowly drifted into a discussion about our fears, anger, hopes, and pain. I did most of the talking. The friend the Lord had provided 24 years ago listened and understood. And then she shared some of the things she had hesitated to share with anyone else. I felt my faith was being bolstered. I was grateful and more than a little awed. God cared enough to even arrange this timely phone call.

The rest of our conversation centered on how awesome our God is to care about such small things in the lives of such unimportant people. Yet, to him, we were important. A section in Luke asks: "Are not five sparrows sold for two pennies? Yet not one of them is forgotten by God. Indeed, the very hairs of your head are all numbered. Don't be afraid; you are worth more than many sparrows" (12:6,7).

After our conversation I could only thank God for providing a wonderful friend. We hadn't solved the problem. Others will have to work on that. But with so much evidence of his caring, it doesn't seem quite so important anymore. Perhaps, with things in a more positive perspective, it's time to share my thoughts with my husband. That's what will be in my prayers tonight. That, and my heartfelt thanks.

CHAPTER TWENTY-THREE

My Child Isn't Listening!

One of the secrets of keeping my sanity when I am stressed is in being able to hand my problems over to the Lord through the gift of prayer. That is where he keeps them until he has made me ready to do something about them.

That said, I wonder where parenting our teenage daughter fits into the above scheme. This much I know: things haven't gone smoothly lately. Recently she stayed at a friend's house, without permission, until midnight. Her normal curfew is 11 P.M. That's when she has our permission to be out, of course.

Her excuse was that she forgot. When we told her that as a consequence she would not be permitted to go out that weekend, her response was, "That's not fair!"

The next morning we asked if her laundry was down. I am certain her answer was yes. Then I discovered a large pile of dirty laundry in the far corner of her bedroom. We've also been encouraging her to invite her new friends over to meet us. So far, no meeting. Perhaps we need to extend the longevity of her latest *consequence* until such time as she brings these friends home to meet us.

Things have been shaky since school started last fall. Quarterly report cards are due next week. When asked what she expects, she is defensive. Another bad sign. She's just barely a teenager, and yet she already thinks she knows more than I do. She acts like I'm the one who should grow up.

What happened to that little girl who enjoyed pleasing her mother and father and teachers and who felt so good about herself when she did? We expressed our concerns to the school guidance counselor, hoping he'd shed some light on her new friends and what's going on at school. He seemed to think I was making a mountain where there might not even be a molehill. As he carefully explained: "All kids go through phases of defiance. It's to be expected."

When asked if he had any suggestions for how to handle it, he suggested we just make up our minds to let her pass through this difficult age. Does that mean there shouldn't be a consequence if she violates her curfew? Does that mean we shouldn't insist on meeting her friends? Does that mean that once she's reached her teens, I have to pick up her laundry?

Somehow, I feel this counselor is on a different channel than we are. Maybe it's even a different planet. Am I making a mountain where there isn't even a molehill? Big problem or little, it's time to search for answers in God's Word.

The most obvious verse for parenting is in Proverbs 22:6. There, through his spokesman, wise King Solomon, God tells his people, "Train a child in the way he should go, and when he is old he will not turn from it." When is the training finished? The guidance counselor seemed to feel that once our daughter was in her teens, more training was fruitless because she refused to accept it.

Searching further, in 1 Samuel 3:13, the Word says, "I told him that I would judge his family forever because of the sin he knew about; his sons made themselves contemptible, and he failed to restrain them." In this text the Lord was talking to Samuel, and he was referring to Eli and Eli's sons, who are described as having "no regard for the LORD" (2:12). Obviously the Lord has some very definite expectations about our obligations as parents.

He also has words for our children: "Do not despise the LORD's discipline and do not resent his rebuke, because the LORD disciplines those he loves, as a father the son he delights in" (Proverbs 3:11,12). I understand that to mean, as parents who love their children, we are to discipline them.

I'm left wondering what to do about the fact that our daughter isn't listening to us any longer and says with both her words as well as her actions: "I've had enough. Now I want to do what I want to do."

It reminds me of the situation in which the father of the prodigal son found himself. The man gave his son what he asked for, and he let him go, even though it was obvious that disaster was imminent. That son represents sinners who turn away from God. Our daughter's behaviors certainly were creating a barrier between her and God.

I wonder how old that prodigal son was? Perhaps this was the type of consequence the counselor had in mind. If so, I feel it's too soon for our daughter. My heart tells me so, and my head agrees. To stop now would be to take the easy way out. God tells us, "Discipline your son, for in that there is hope; do not be a willing party to his death" (Proverbs 19:18).

During the years and months we have left with our daughter, and while there is still a chance to help her turn her actions back to God-pleasing behaviors, it seems our job as parents is to keep trying to train our child in the way she should go. Only when she is old enough to legally leave our home will the formal training stop. Then, as always, we will keep her in our prayers.

God does add that when she is old, she will not depart from the lessons she learned while she was growing up. Our job as parents? To keep training our children in his Word. To keep trying.

Perhaps we also need to remind our daughter: "He who spares the rod hates his son, but he who loves him is careful to discipline him" (Proverbs 13:24) and "No discipline seems pleasant at the time, but painful. Later, however, [such discipline] produces a harvest of righteousness and peace for those who have been trained by it" (Hebrews 12:11). That's our prayer for the child who isn't listening.

CHAPTER TWENTY-FOUR

The Harvest Awaits

"A man reaps what he sows" (Galatians 6:7). Today my crop hasn't been very good. While getting ready to give my personal witness in a telephone interview for a Christian radio talk show, I yelled at one daughter whose passive defiance is legendary. She was sleeping in when our family needed her to be up, helping.

While relaxing for a few minutes after the talk show, I managed to waste an entire hour playing computer games. Later, while talking with an adult daughter, I just didn't feel like being sympathetic about her personal issues, so I didn't encourage her to tell me more when it was obvious she really needed to do so.

What is it that Paul says in Romans 7:15,19? "I do not understand what I do. For what I want to do I do not do, but what I hate I do. For what I do is not the good I want to do; no, the evil I do not want to do—this I keep on doing."

My children are usually willing to admit that they don't have a perfect mother. Some days I wouldn't even qualify as a reasonably good mother. One son often reminds me of this; and he considers himself an expert on moms because he's had more than the usual number of moms walk through his life. Almost all of them have also walked out of his life again. Occasionally, I even envy the *out-going*. (More proof of my state of imperfection.)

So how does someone this hopeless get back on track? Eating is one of my favorite pastimes. Even if the kids weren't reminding me it was dinnertime, I'd listen to my stomach and provide supper for them . . . and me, eventually. However, getting back on track spiritually can be more difficult.

Drifting away from the Word is sadly quite easy. Getting back into God's Word and becoming more open to a change in my own heart is always the hard part. But I've done this a lot through the years (told you I wasn't perfect) and have developed my own get-back-to-his-peace routine.

My first step is prayer. Not the quick "Lord, help" but an ongoing, daylong prayer time that is in session wherever I am. On the road picking kids up from school, in the laundry room making a path, pushing the vacuum into that far corner that no one else can find, or even while creating a new bulletin board display as a volunteer for Calvary Academy, I keep up a silent dialogue with the Lord. I keep it silent because people tend to look at you strangely if you do this out loud, and their looks can be a distraction.

I generally don't use this prayer time to ask the Lord for things. Instead, I make it a time to ask him to bring me closer to him. This is a time to ask for a deeper, stronger faith. And he promises that I will get it. "Ask and it will be given to you; seek and you will find; knock and the door will be opened to you. For everyone who asks receives; he who seeks finds; and to him who knocks, the door will be opened" (Matthew 7:7,8).

The second step is a purposeful step. And it too is based on faith. I know the Lord loves me in spite of my shortcomings. After all, "God so loved the world that he gave his one and only Son, that whoever believes in him shall not perish but have eternal life. For God did not send his Son into the world to condemn the world, but to save the world through him" (John 3:16,17). Recognizing this means that I can use my time to step back and take a look at my actions and inactions and then offer my praise to God for all that's going on, both positive and negative. When I am truly putting every part of my life into God's hands for him to control, I am at peace. Sometimes the peace is short-lived, especially when I begin thinking of me again instead of his will, working in me. It's then that I need to refocus on God again and on all that he has done for me.

Satan is good at finding ways to make us feel guilty. It's one of his best tricks. His purpose is to distract us. But there is a godly way of fighting him. Instead of wringing my hands and beating myself up for my shortcomings, I praise God and thank him for using even a nothing like me to further his kingdom.

With God, it's all a matter of timing. And God's timing is always perfect. "At just the right time, when we were still powerless, Christ died for the ungodly" (Romans 5:6). "The one who sows to please his sinful nature, from that nature will reap destruction; the one who sows to please the Spirit, from the Spirit will reap eternal life. Let us not become weary in doing good, for at the proper time we will reap a harvest if we do not give up" (Galatians 6:8,9). That's my goal: to keep sowing to please God's Spirit, knowing that at the proper time there's a glorious harvest waiting.

CHAPTER TWENTY-FIVE

Strength to the Weary

I woke up this morning and everything looked great. A couple manuscripts awaited finishing touches. A friend was coming to supplement her income and save my sanity by digging into some long-neglected housecleaning projects. The kids were up and out of bed on time . . . and their beds were made! It was going to be a great day.

Then the phone rang.

Fifteen minutes later, as I hung up the receiver, my thoughts hovered between anger, frustration, discouragement, and the feeling that maybe I should just quit. Being a foster parent was not fun. Being a foster parent was just a setup for disappointment. Being a foster parent meant watching kids get hurt again when these same kids had already been hurt more than most adults ever are—kids who have no defensive strategies left other than antisocial behaviors.

Regulations, rules, guidelines—all made by adults—were created with someone's personal agenda. Some of these adults have never even spoken with a child crying out for permanency. Few have given thought to how these children feel. They each come with their own biases, furthered by questionable conclusions. Never mind that the social workers who do see these kids have concluded these methods aren't working. Never mind that the foster and adoptive moms and dads who have to comply with these methodologies have agreed that by the time they have them figured out, new rules are being introduced that are even more impossible. Never mind that the children these rules are supposed to protect are finding themselves living in the temporary foster care settings for longer and longer periods, instead of with families committed to keeping them forever.

Yes, I understand that there must be guidelines. But why not look to the needs of each child and then, with flexible guidelines, make decisions based on individual needs?

Here's an example. The current guidelines have been interpreted to mean that a brother and sister will have to be separated because there cannot be more than eight children in a foster home . . . and we already have seven children under the age of 18. Why aren't there ways to bend these guidelines when it's in the best interest of the child? Everyone has already agreed this would be one of the rare times when that would make some sense. That is, everyone except the top man who signs the foster care license.

If we do turn out to be temporary, all the more reason to keep them together. That's my opinion. But this fellow isn't listening.

Standing at the window, watching my kids start a game of baseball, I feel beaten, and I hear myself say: "I'm tired, Lord. Did you ever get tired?"

Looking for something more productive to do than stand there feeling sorry for myself, I look in my Bible's concordance under *tired*. There's something in John 4:6. I read, "Jacob's well was there, and Jesus, tired as he was from the journey, sat down by the well." We know that the Pharisees had gotten upset with Jesus shortly before this and that Jesus had walked a long way that day. It seems clear, though, that his exhaustion was more physical than emotional—another indication that Jesus truly was human. But my question was this: Does God tire in the same way that I get tired?

One answer is found in Isaiah 40:28-31: "The LORD is the everlasting God, the Creator of the ends of the earth. He will not grow tired or weary, and his understanding no one can fathom. He gives strength to the weary and increases the power of the weak. Even youths grow tired and weary, and young men stumble and fall; but those who hope in the LORD will renew their strength. They will soar on wings like eagles; they will run and not grow weary, they will walk and not be faint."

The Lord not only gives us sleep at night to replenish our physical strength, but he's right there with us, able and willing to help us deal with our emotional exhaustion too. He knows when we're going to get upset. He knows when we're getting tired. He knows when we're discouraged by things like unfair rules and bureaucracy. He knows, and in his all-knowing way, he promises, not that it won't happen but rather that, when it does, those who hope in the Lord will renew their strength.

Remembering another verse in Matthew, I read, "Come to me, all you who are weary and burdened, and I will give you rest" (11:28). The Lord gives strength to the weary and increases the power of the weak. Perhaps I should find out the appeal procedure.

It's going to be another great day.

CHAPTER TWENTY-SIX

Words, Not Actions

We have a daughter who has a unique way of smiling and saying yes to our requests and suggestions, and to the outward eye is in total compliance; then, when no one is watching, she does nothing. She's practiced her art to the point that if she were competing in the Olympics, she'd get a perfect 10. The psychology books call it *passive defiance.* We call it hard to live with.

The cause? With this particular 16-year-old, it is probably the result of too often being left to fend for herself from the time she was a toddler up through her early years of grade school. If she was hungry, she would tell a neighbor and the neighbor would feed her. If she was cold, she'd tell another neighbor and that neighbor would let her come in to warm up and play. By the time she was old enough to attend school, she said whatever was necessary to please the teacher and get herself off the hook.

During her years in the foster care system, she continued her pattern, telling the social worker everything she knew the social worker wanted to hear, telling her therapist the things she knew her therapist would like to hear, telling her teacher the things she wanted to hear. When she got home, she told her foster mother the things that would please her. The rest of the time our daughter did whatever she felt like doing.

What happened when problems surfaced? In her mind, problems resulted from other people's behaviors, not hers! She told her teacher she didn't get her homework done because she had to go to therapy. She claimed she couldn't get an assignment finished because her social worker had come to say they might have a permanent family for her. She didn't have lunch money because her foster mother forgot to give it to her. (Actually, the money was in her pocket, earmarked for spending on a huge candy bar she'd seen at the drugstore.) She told her social worker she was doing great in everything and had lots of friends, except for the one mean girl who didn't like her and wouldn't let some of the kids be her friends. What she didn't tell the social worker was that the mean girl was upset because our daughter had borrowed her calculator, taken it home, and now claimed she never had it.

She told her foster mother that she had paid for her lunch ticket, but the teacher must have forgotten to mark it down. The list went on and on.

By the time this girl joined our family through adoption at age ten, her "coping technique" was entrenched. In her eyes, all she needed to do to get out of an uncomfortable situation, whether it be dishes, homework, or being held responsible for being disrespectful to an authority figure, was to come up with some reason that made it clear that nothing was ever her fault. She was always the victim. She shouldn't have to do lunch dishes because she hadn't used any when she ate. She shouldn't have to do homework because the teacher failed to explain it clearly. She was angry with her adoptive mom when asked to turn off the TV after two continuous hours of watching because her birth mother had never treated her very well. She had an answer for every situation. And after six years of hearing them, we couldn't help wishing she'd use that creativity in a little different way. We even wondered if it might be possible that she had manipulated her views about things so much with her own words that she was no longer able to identify the truth. Had she been filtering everything through the sieve of her own distorted logic for so long that it was impossible for her to see life in a way that was honest?

She talked long and hard about it with her Christian teachers because it really was a problem in the classroom. She talked long and hard about it with her teen Bible study leader. She talked long and hard about it with her pastor. We shared Paul's words in Acts 26:20: "I preached that they should repent and turn to God and prove their repentance by their deeds."

The words of James 2:17-22 applied so well that we had to talk about them. "Faith by itself, if it is not accompanied by action, is dead. . . . Show me your faith without deeds, and I will show you my faith by what I do. . . . [Abraham's] faith and his actions were working together, and his faith was made complete by what he did."

After all these years, there are days when I think she is finally starting to get it. Then, without warning, the old tape kicks back in, and once again we're living with passive defiance. It's evident when her words are not matched by her actions.

"Please fold the towels and bring them upstairs."

"Yes, Mom."

Two hours later the towels are still in the dryer. Now the question becomes, Do I have the stamina today to confront her so she learns to follow through, or should I take the easy way out and do it myself?

"Please bring your laundry down to be washed."

"Yes, Mom."

As I finish the last load in the laundry room, I realize none of them are her clothes.

"Please leave your work schedule on the refrigerator so I know when you need rides."

"Yes, Mom, right away."

Guess what isn't there two days later. Guess who's indignant and angry when I dare to ask for it again because I feel some responsibility for getting her to work on time.

Yet, we are seeing some improvements. The schedule will eventually appear on the refrigerator door . . . after the anger passes. The laundry will find its way to the laundry room, and she's learning to operate the washer. The towels will eventually find their way to the bathrooms.

I can thankfully say that the passive defiance isn't present as often as it once was. Her anger is sometimes more controlled—enough that we can have a discussion. Sometimes I even find homework completed before I check on it.

She tells me that remembering to pray before she speaks makes a big difference. I can see the results of that in her actions.

Perhaps it's time for me to learn by her example.

CHAPTER TWENTY-SEVEN

A Time for Rules

As with all families, ours has a few rules. From my angle, it is good to have as few rules as possible. From my kids' angle, we have rules, rules, and more rules. However, after carefully scrutinizing each rule, I can assure you that they are all necessary. Some examples of the rules of our house include:

- No roughhousing in the kitchen or the living room.
- If you break your bed, you sleep on the floor.
- He who wants money, works. Chores are everywhere.
- Table manners must come to dinner.
- Need a ride? Be nice to the driver.
- Wash your dishes in hot water.
- Baths are necessary after bathing the dog.
- Muddy shoes stay outside.
- Mothers are not meant to retrieve Frisbees or kites.
- If you didn't bake it, you can't eat it without asking.

It's amazing, to me anyway, that sometimes my kids object to these rules. But when I think about it, that's probably just human nature. We break God's rules, the Ten Commandments, every day. Of course, there are those people who declare that rules are meant to be broken, especially in our changing times. For example, the Sixth Commandment—You should not commit adultery—is declared by some to be outdated in our liberated society. Yet to what does this liberate us?

Articles in newspapers and magazines continually cite statistics indicating that venereal diseases are running rampant. Then, of course, there is AIDS, caused by the HIV virus and often passed through sexual contact. One needs only to turn on the TV and surf through stations to find extramarital affairs being portrayed as the norm. One aspect of living in a liberated society that is not often talked about is the emotional pain inflicted by breaking this commandment. There's always a price to be paid, now or later. There's a good reason why some of us shake our heads at the callous way infidelity is treated these days.

I guess on closer analysis every one of God's commandments is broken on a regular basis. And if we aren't breaking a particular commandment, our human inclination is to judge those who are.

Perhaps it's too painful to look at those we do break. Coveting probably happens every time we hear of someone winning the lottery. Doesn't bearing false witness occur if I listen to gossip and don't try to set the record straight? Honoring your father and mother: How many times have I not called or driven over to my mother's when my conscience said I should? Worship: Lenten services are sometimes not convenient. See what I mean? Even trying hard to avoid these pitfalls, I so often fall short. All of us can relate to Paul's sentiments in Romans 7:18-20: "I know that nothing good lives in me, that is, in my sinful nature. For I have the desire to do what is good, but I cannot carry it out. For what I do is not the good I want to do; no, the evil I do not want to do—this I keep on doing. Now if I do what I do not want to do, it is no longer I who does it, but it is sin living in me that does it."

Even Saint Paul had trouble with his sinful flesh. So, I'm in good company. But the company that I really would like to be keeping is with Christ Jesus. That's a degree of perfection impossible to reach on our own.

Oh, how badly we need a Savior! Christ had to come to fulfill the law when it was impossible for us to keep God's law perfectly. How thankful we can be for that great gift! How glad I am that he didn't give up on saving me! That's a good example to follow when I become determined not to give up on my children.

So, let's review the ten rules God gave us, starting with Jesus' words in Matthew 22:37-39: " 'Love the Lord your God with all your heart and with all your soul and with all your mind.' This is the first and greatest commandment. And the second is like it: 'Love your neighbor as yourself.' "

Well, maybe we don't need more after all. These will suffice.

CHAPTER TWENTY-EIGHT

A Dialogue with the Lord

Recently someone asked what I mean when I encourage others to "pray continually." My explanation, "Just start talking to God and stop to listen every so often," was received with a look of skepticism. The other day when I found myself carrying on a dialogue with the Lord, I wrote it down, figuring that showing is better than telling. The occasion for this prayer involved a minor confrontation with a rebellious son.

Lord, help! What do I do with such a rebellious child? I want to help him; we've prayed continually for him since he came to our family. Nothing seems to change his heart. He is so angry. He refuses to take responsibility for his decisions or his actions. And when he's confronted with them he becomes angry and vents his anger on his teacher or us.

He's angry because his birth father couldn't take care of him. He's angry because his little sister was adopted by her foster family, who didn't want a child his age. He's angry because the family before us didn't adopt him, even though they promised they would. His anger probably scared them. He's angry because he thinks everybody's telling him what to do, and he doesn't want to be told what to do.

So how do you deal with rebellion, Lord? You've dealt with it for a long time, haven't you, going way back to your first kids, Adam and Eve. Finally had to throw them out of paradise, didn't you! On the other hand, that wasn't as much for punishment as it was for their own protection. After they ate the fruit that opened their eyes to right and wrong, you didn't want them to make matters worse by giving them the chance to eat the fruit of eternal life. At least this way—your way—we can die physically and still live spiritually for eternity.

In the epistle of James the subject of anger comes up. One text says, "Be quick to listen, slow to speak and slow to become angry, for man's anger does not bring about the righteous life that God desires" (1:19). In other words, I had better be careful not to let my feelings of frustration and anger feed my son's anger so that his anger becomes even more entrenched. As a parent, my job is to be a role model so he knows, by example, the best way to handle his anger. Actions speak louder than words. Somewhere I remember reading that. Lord, help me remember that.

In another book, you've told us, "'In your anger do not sin': Do not let the sun go down while you are still angry, and do not give the devil a foothold" (Ephesians 4:26,27). We'd better continue helping our son work on his anger so that anger doesn't lead to more rebellion. "God is merciful and forgiving, even though we have rebelled against him" (Daniel 9:9).

Hopefully someday my son will pray along with us, "Remember not the sins of my youth and my rebellious ways" (Psalm 25:7).

I appreciate your listening, Lord. Thanks for helping me see things a little clearer. And thanks for sending your Son so that my son can deal with his anger and live with hope.

CHAPTER TWENTY-NINE

R & R

Me? Travel alone? Be away from home for a whole week to visit our son Craig and his family? How could I possibly be gone for a whole week? Yes, I could use some rest and relaxation.

Now, Bob is very capable of caring for our children. It's just that we haven't done this role reversal thing for such a length of time. We have done it for a couple days, when I was speaking at retreats or seminars. But that was different. Then it was the Lord's work. This isn't the Lord's work. This is for me. Just for me.

Seeing Craig and Gretchen and Justin, Katie, and Naomi would be wonderful. They live so far away—six hours by plane. Our grandchildren are growing up, and we don't see them often enough. The "big kids," Craig and Gretchen, are fun to be with too. Even when we're solving the most serious problems and some of us are in tears, it's still wonderful just to be together.

I would also have to admit that things have been quite intense for me here lately. I suppose it has something to do with being a mom of such a large family at Christmas time. The other day a lady politely asked if we buy gifts for all 25 of our kids at Christmas. I almost snapped at her, "No, we buy for half of them on alternate years." Of course we get gifts for each of them, for their wives or husbands, and for our grandchildren. That's what moms and dads and grandmas and grandpas do. Our gifts may not be as expensive as the gifts other families give. Rather, I start early, plan carefully, and do a lot of creative things. So far no one's indicated a feeling of being deprived. In fact, we've even asked ourselves if we're overindulging and discussed how we can make sure our emphasis stays on Christ. It's a matter of priorities. After Christ comes family. Then comes me.

Maybe it's time to look at it from that angle. It would certainly be okay with Christ if I spent time with part of my family we don't get to see very often. That's it. I've exhausted my reasons not to go.

So there—a time for R and R can be justified. I don't need to feel guilty. Still, traveling without Bob will be different. Our travel times together have always been renewal times—getting reacquainted times. We both look forward to them and treasure them long afterwards. In traveling alone I would miss that.

What would I do for six hours? A list of possibilities could include:

Read a book (without interruptions).

Write another chapter of my book (without interruptions).

Eat at my own pace (without interruptions).

Watch people.

Pray for the people I'm watching.

Pray for the family I've left at home.

Pray for the husband I've left to cope with the family I've left at home.

Sit and think (without interruptions).

Doesn't sound too bad. Bob's suggestion might have merit. The final "convincer" comes with our doctor's diagnosis of my lingering (two-plus months) light rash as a skin condition often caused by emotional stress in women my age (between 30 and 60). Obviously, I haven't been handling some days too well, so maybe it is time to relax and rejuvenate my emotional and spiritual life.

Christmas comes, and Christmas Day passes. The day after Christmas, I find myself winging westward. I am duly greeted at Portland's airport: "Grandma! Grandma!" The regaling comes from six-year-old Justin and four-year-old Katie. Their joyful welcome makes me soar even higher than flying in the jet. Then two-year-old Naomi, who can't possibly remember me, emboldened by her excited older siblings, says, "Grandma!" and gives me a hug too. This is going to be fun!

The six of us spend the next several days catching up, moving on in our relationships. I stand in awe of the parenting skills my son and daughter-in-law have cultivated and find myself wondering if I had any part in this. I can see already that they are better parents than I was. My son has learned well from his earthly father, as well as his heavenly Father. My daughter-in-law has also learned well from her parents.

While not perfect, my grandchildren measure very high on the wonderful scale. And I wish I could give them every possible happiness. Yet happiness, like faith, is something they will need to find for themselves. The best I can do is share mine. It dawns on me, that's the best I can do for my sons and daughters still living at home.

I wonder how Bob and the kids are doing.

An e-mail arrives. Its title: "Status of the Wasser House."

> Looks like we have another storm on the way. I went out and bought a new thermostat for the living room. Well, it works very well, but it started to smoke right away. So I read the directions and found that the repairman had wired the other one white to red and red to white. That's why we kept on smelling smoke and hearing it hiss all the time. All I did was put the wires back to the same position in which I had found them.

> Now it turns out that's not the whole problem. When I turned the wires around, I accidentally broke the lead-in wire from the furnace. So I called the electrician to come and fix it. I hope that he gets here before spring. I tried!

> Hope all is well with you. I put a new zone valve on the above, but don't worry. The kitchen stove still works when we need heat.

We laughed.

I decide to finish out my stay with the hope that things will have cooled down by the time I get home. Craig and I relive the time he and his father purchased a beautiful, antique chandelier for $3 at a garage sale. They hung it in our dining room. It worked for 30 seconds before the sizzle and pop that blew the breakers. The electrician was able to make the chandelier work even after the fire, so I'm sure he'll do fine with the thermostat.

A day later I send my lighthearted reply to Bob's e-mail, suggesting I could be persuaded to stay even longer if he wanted me to. By return e-mail (the thought crosses my mind, "If he's on the Internet, who's watching the kids?"), Bob says: "Sure. No problem."

I have to admit that I miss all of them and my rash is almost gone. I'll leave tomorrow as planned. Besides, I suspect Bob was setting me up. He knows I'm too cheap to pay extra to change my ticket. It's nice to know I'll be returning not only with a greater appreciation for them but also to their greater appreciation of me. Bob is good at *soloing,* but I'm a better everyday chef. Perhaps this R and R thing has merit, especially if done often enough.

On the trip home I decide to try a mini version of this R and R concept every day. It'll be a time of relaxation and reflection, a time of saying thanks for what is and a time of asking for the Lord's peace. After all, we know that "the peace of God, which transcends all understanding, will guard [our] hearts and [our] minds in Christ Jesus" (Philippians 4:7).

I think I know now why I got the rash.

In His Time

I went shopping for a dress for Tanya and Paul's wedding the other day. I told the salesclerks I was looking for something that would make me look thin, sexy, and glamorous. Not one of them had the courage to tell me it was too late.

I have had the same timidity on many occasions—but usually in regard to more serious subjects. When my father died at age 54, we had been given time to prepare for it. He was ill the last four years of his life. And we understood that our time with him was limited. That time of preparation made it possible for me to say things that were difficult to say in our stoic German-American family. Things like telling him how I loved him and how much we appreciated everything he had done for us . . . and how much he meant to me.

On the day before he died, I drove over to sit with him so that my mother could take a much-needed nap. (How thankful I am even today for the neighbor who watched my kids that day so I could be with my dad!) That day he reassured me that God was going to take care of my mother and little sister. He was sure of this because God had always taken the time to reassure him. And now my father was taking whatever time he had left to reassure me.

Bob and I received a letter the other day from our daughter-in-law Lisa. Her father died last year with no warning after having a sudden heart attack. She addressed her thank-you letter to us on Valentines Day, telling us how much she loved our son and how greatly she appreciated the Christian influence we have had on him. She wanted to take the time to tell us this before it was too late. And she did.

The point is that we need to use the available time God gives us to communicate the things that are most important to the people who mean the most to us in our lives. I know all this. I've seen how it works. And yet, too often, I'm reluctant to share these things that need to be said. I rationalize: "They know Christ. They've known his love since they were children. They've attended church regularly. They've studied the Bible stories and learned their catechism." Some have not continued their daily walks with God. They know I'm concerned about that. But after I've said it a couple times, I find myself reluctant to keep telling them. Instead, I find myself praying for them, "Keep them safe in your love, Lord Jesus."

If one of them were trapped in a burning house, I'd surely give up my life to save that child. Why, then, am I so reluctant to talk with my dearest treasures in life about eternity and their Savior from sin?

Perhaps I should write a prayer and hang it above my computer to be read on a daily basis. Something like "Give me strength, Lord. Give me courage. Give me wisdom. And give these to me at the right time to share your saving truth with those I love."